Technical Writing in the Corporate World

Understanding, Developing, and Editing Technical Documents

Herman A. Estrin, Ph.D.
Norbert Elliot, Ph.D.

A FIFTY-MINUTE™ SERIES BOOK

1-800-442-7477 • 25 Thomson Place, Boston MA • www.courseilt.com

Technical Writing in the Corporate World

Understanding, Developing, and Editing Technical Documents

Herman A. Estrin, Ph.D.
Norbert Elliot, Ph.D.

New Jersey Institue of Technology

CREDITS
Editor: **Anne Knight**
Design and Typesetting: **Interface Studio**
Cover Design: **Nicole Phillips**
Artwork: **Ralph Mapson**

ISBN 1-56052-004-3
Library of Congress Catalog Card Number 89-81249
Printed in Canada by Webcom Limited
5 6 7 8 PM 06 05 04

LEARNING OBJECTIVES FOR:

TECHNICAL WRITING IN THE CORPORATE WORLD

The objectives for *Technical Writing in the Corporate World* are listed below. They have been developed to guide you, the reader, to the core issues covered in this book.

Objectives

❑   1) **To present general principles of excellence in technical writing**

❑   2) **To discuss procedures for specific types of writing**

❑   3) **To explain correctness in technical writing**

Assessing Your Progress

In addition to the learning objectives above, Course Technology has developed a Crisp Series **assessment** that covers the fundamental information presented in this book. A 25-item, multiple-choice and true/false questionnaire allows the reader to evaluate his or her comprehension of the subject matter. To buy the assessment and answer key, go to www.courseilt.com and search on the book title or via the assessment format, or call 1-800-442-7477.

Assessments should not be used in any employee selection process.

ACKNOWLEDGMENTS

In writing this book, we realized our debt to the organizations where we have worked as consultants and writers over the years. Especially, we wish to thank the following: E&E Cruz Construction Company, FMC Corporation, International Telephone and Telegraph—Defense Communications Division, Johnson and Michaels, Lone Star Gas Company, New Jersey Department of Transportation, Pilot Metal Fabricators, RCA American Communications, RCA Astro Labs, Schoor, DePalma, and Canger, United Jersey Banks, and Zozzaro Industries. We would also like to thank our students at the New Jersey Institute of Technology for making us better teachers of technical writing. John Opie, Director of the Center for Technology Studies at the New Jersey Institute of Technology, served as an excellent critical reader.

This work is dedicated to Pearl, Karen, and Robert Estrin and for Lorna Jean, Christian, Luke, Jesse, Nicholas, and Sophia Elliot.

CONTENTS

(Continued next page)

CONTENTS (Continued)

SECTION 1

UNDERSTANDING
TECHNICAL WRITING

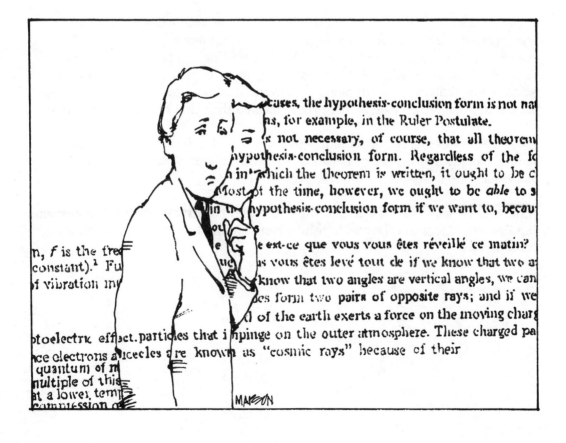

1.0 UNDERSTANDING TECHNICAL WRITING

WHAT IS TECHNICAL WRITING?

Developed by the Sumerians in Mesopotamia about 3500 B.C., writing is a relatively recent invention, especially when we consider that human beings have been on earth approximately 50,000 years. Some scholars suggest that writing was developed to help individuals exchange goods, and so writing may also be understood as instrumental in the development of commerce. If we see writing as a technology, we begin to demystify it; that is, we begin to realize that the ability to write is a craft that can be learned.

However, many sophisticated and intelligent individuals in industry and government believe that writing is a special skill, a sort of gift magically given to some. This view of writing is very harmful because it implies that the ability to write effectively is beyond the capacity of some. It is fundamental, therefore, that *you begin to see yourself as a writer.*

Precision and creativity in writing do not depend on the publication of short stories or on the possession of a degree in English. Engineers, architects, computer scientists—all are interested in clear writing. As Nobel Prize winner Arno A. Penzias argues, there are few things more important than educating scientists as writers. Without being able to put our thoughts on paper, he believes we cannot operate on a level more sophisticated than that of a preliterate tribe.

How may we define the important activity of technical writing? Simply, it is *writing that explains technology to various technical, organizational, and societal audiences.*

More will be said about the role of the audience in technical writing in a moment, but first it is important for you to think carefully about your attitudes toward writing.

1.1 SURVEYING YOUR ATTITUDES TOWARD WRITING

Because of unique experiences both within and outside of school, you have probably developed certain feelings about writing. Which attitudes will serve you well, and which will inhibit your development as a writer?

Next to each of the statements below, circle whether you *agree, don't know,* or *disagree* with each statement. Comments on each statement will follow.

1. I find writing difficult.

    Agree   *Don't Know*   *Disagree*

2. If I could only remember the rules of grammar, I would become a better writer.

    Agree   *Don't Know*   *Disagree*

3. If a colleague can write a successful academic essay, then that colleague will be able to write a successful technical document.

    Agree   *Don't Know*   *Disagree*

4. If a colleague speaks well, then that colleague will surely be a good writer.

    Agree   *Don't Know*   *Disagree*

5. Technical documents are always objective.

    Agree   *Don't Know*   *Disagree*

6. Technical documents are never argumentative.

    Agree   *Don't Know*   *Disagree*

7. Because I know the activities of everyone in my office, I don't need to write that much.

    Agree   *Don't Know*   *Disagree*

8. Although I often have trouble writing down my ideas, I know exactly what I mean.

    Agree   *Don't Know*   *Disagree*

9. An outline is the best way to organize a technical document.

    Agree   *Don't Know*   *Disagree*

10. My role as a technical expert comes first. My role as a writer comes second.

    Agree   *Don't Know*   *Disagree*

AUTHORS' COMMENTS: YOUR ATTITUDES TOWARD WRITING

1. Writing is difficult. If you find writing difficult, then you are in good company. Some of the best technical writers find writing to be a demanding, exacting task. These writers, however, are not paralyzed when they must document a technical procedure for other specialists or translate specialized information to an audience of non-specialists. There is, then, a distinction to be drawn: while you may find writing difficult, your apprehension should not be so great that you are unable to convey your ideas.

2. Remembering the rules of grammar will not make you an effective writer. In 1986, a study funded by the National Institute of Education examined over 2,000 publications dealing with research on writing. The researchers could find no evidence that the study of grammar or mechanics improved writing processes or products. In fact, some studies indicated that an over-concern with grammar during the drafting process may inhibit an individual's ability to compose. Of course, this finding does not mean that standard usage is not an important part of communications, but there is substantial research indicating that an ability to identify parts of speech does not, by itself, produce good writing. You must begin to think about writing not merely as the sum of your grammatical knowledge but as a dynamic process incorporating discovery, organization, and revision. (More about the writing process will be discussed in Section 1.3.)

3. Academic writing is different from nonacademic writing. Although the anthropological term ''discourse communities'' may be unfamiliar to you, it conveys the fact that different professions value different elements of writing. An electrical engineer, for example, may work to create a lead for a memo that can be read in three seconds, while a literary essayist may craft an introduction that extends over three paragraphs. Our point: technical writing is special. It requires an ability to render the complex world of modern technology to a variety of audiences never imagined in the traditional classroom. So different is the corporation from the academy that many successful writers in government and industry tell us that they had to re-train themselves (as you are doing now) to write for the world of work.

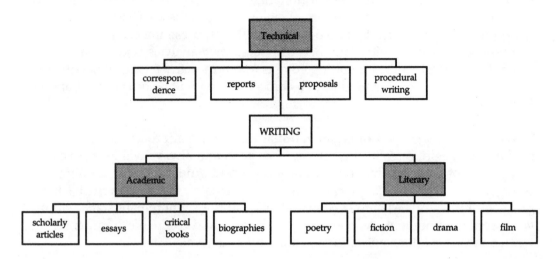

Figure 1. Three Worlds of Writing

In Figure 1 the three worlds of writing are identified. Take a moment to think about how these worlds are similar and different. What is your attitude towards technical, academic, and literary writing?

4. Just because you are an effective speaker does not mean you are an effective writer. Speaking well and writing well do not necessarily go hand-in-hand. When you speak, you can use your voice in a number of ways to help you convey information; you can go back and repeat a complex point; and you can answer questions as they are raised by your audience. None of these advantages is possible in the case of writing. The page itself is silent, and you must be skilled to convey on a page what you can convey naturally with your voice. Difficult points must be explained as they arise because you will not be sitting alongside each reader as your document is reviewed. Remember: speaking is natural, but writing is a learned behavior, a technology.

5. No one can be completely objective. Early theorists of technical writing assumed that technical writing must always be objective. Later, theorists have come to realize the impossibility of achieving complete objectivity. The choice of a statistical method or the interpretation of its complex result, for instance, both involve the subjective judgment of the scientist. This acknowledgment of subjectivity does not mean, however, that writers are free to obscure information for their own purposes. Instead, the challenge of technical writing is for writers to be aware of their biases and still present a balanced view.

AUTHORS' COMMENTS (Continued)

6. Technical documents are often argumentative. A civil engineer trying to solve a rapid transit problem in a large urban city and a systems analyst proposing a word processing program to a corporation, will both present a claim and substantiate that claim with data. Because persuasive analysis is key in a technological marketplace, a cutting edge is found in many technical documents. (The usefulness of argumentation in technical writing will be further examined in Section 2.3)

7. Writing is a major part of organizational life. As we approach the 21st century, we begin to realize that change has been and always will be a permanent component of corporate life. (Note: For an excellent guide to understanding change, order *Understanding Organizational Change* using the form in the back of this book.) It is unrealistic to believe that all conditions will remain static within your work environment. As people shift positions and companies reorganize, the written record is often central to the company's survival.

8. Writing is a great aid to thinking. Have you ever had the experience of writing your ideas down, reading them, and realizing that the words on the page fail to carry your message? As you begin to revise, perhaps you notice that your process of writing is making you think more precisely. Only when you are finished composing the document do you feel that you truly understand the problem at hand. If this process is familiar to you, then you have experienced a great benefit of writing: it makes you think more carefully. As literacy theorist Walter Ong puts it, "writing helps us restructure our consciousness." So, although you may have some sense of what you want to say, writing will enable you to organize and to clarify your thoughts.

9. There are many ways to plan a document. Outlining is certainly one helpful way of organizing ideas; yet there are other ways. You may begin to organize your document by freewriting your ideas and then by linking them together, or you may draw the plan of your document by creating a web of ideas emanating from a central idea. Some writers even begin by creating a series of questions which readers may pose and then draft the documents by responding to these questions.

10. Technical experts must be able to express their ideas in writing. There is no question that your technical expertise is central to your job. Your ability to convey your expertise is nevertheless also important. Your view of yourself becomes most complete when you think of yourself as not only a producer of technical information but also a provider of technical innovation.

1.2 KNOWING YOUR AUDIENCE

All writing exists within specific contexts. Whether you are working in private industry or in government, your organization has its own way of communicating information.

Central to success in your organization is your ability to serve the needs of your readers. From the non-specialist to the specialist, audiences vary enormously. Often there will be multiple readers for a single document, and it is not uncommon for sections of a report to be read by different readers, each with different expertise, interests, and responsibilities. How can you serve the various needs of your readers?

It is helpful to think of technical writing as a process of translation. Figure 2 will help you visualize the translation process:

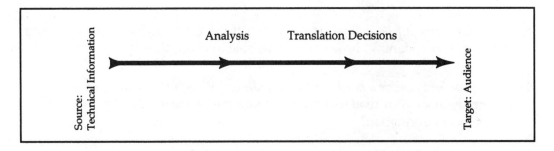

Figure 2. The Process of Technical Translation

The *source* is the technical information that you know. As you begin to *analyze* your information, you begin to decide which information will—and will not—be significant to your audience. After you identify which information is most significant, you begin to make *translation decisions* in order to adapt your information to the *target,* your audience.

KNOWING YOUR AUDIENCE (Continued)

Here are five questions you can ask yourself when you must communicate technical information to your audience:

1. *What is my purpose in writing?* Are you writing to inform or to convince your audience? What do you hope to achieve with your document?

2. *What do your readers know?* Are your readers knowledgeable about the information you will present, or do you need to spend time presenting a brief narrative context for your information?

3. *What do your readers need to know?* Is a detailed report needed, or will a brief, informative memo do the job? Since your readers may use the information you present to write their own reports, how can you make sure that your document is accurate?

4. *Are there any pitfalls that you should avoid?* If there are any potential problems that you can identify, how will you be able to avoid these problems?

5. *How can you achieve a bond with your audience?* Which strategies can you employ to let your readers know that you are on their side in providing technical information?

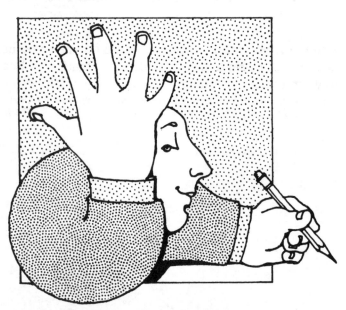

FIVE QUESTIONS TO ASK YOURSELF

SIX TECHNIQUES FOR SUCCESS

Besides these five questions, there are a number of techniques that will prove useful to you in presenting technical information:

1. DEFINE TERMINOLOGY. Certain key terms will be common to anyone who works in your immediate group. In the morning, a group leader in a nuclear power plant may write a memo to a colleague about a projected start-up date for the 809 MWe BWR. When a reporter for the local newspaper arrives for an interview that afternoon, however, the group leader must be prepared to chat about the first day of operation of the 809 megawatt electric boiling water reactor, a nuclear facility that will provide .809 billion watts of power.

2. USE SHORT, WELL-WRITTEN SENTENCES. The more complex the information, the shorter your sentences should be. Read this excerpt from a chemical engineer to a colleague:

> Three separate filtration, washing, and dewatering problems that occur in the production of Herbicide 773 are considered in detail in the enclosed study which was made on a small, continuous drum-type filter, and the results are believed to be adequate to predict the behavior of small scale equipment and to afford a basis for the selection of larger units for new production plants.

Now note the difference that shorter sentences make:

> The enclosed paper analyzes three separate filtration, washing, and dewatering problems occurring in the production of Herbicide 773. This study was made with a small, drum-type filter. The results are believed to be adequate to predict the behavior of small scale equipment. Therefore, the study will afford a basis for the selection of larger units for new production plants.

3. USE BRIEF PARAGRAPHS. Instead of using paragraphs that ramble on line after line, craft concise, well-structured paragraphs. The reader will then be able to follow you because of the "rest" afforded by effective use of white space.

4. STRIVE FOR COHERENCE. Be sure that your writing allows no place where the reader might become lost. Adverbial conjunctions such as those below will help your readers follow the logic of your writing.

> consequently, finally, furthermore, hence, however, indeed, instead, moreover, nevertheless, otherwise, therefore.

(For more information on coherence, see Section 1.4; for more information on adverbial conjunctions using with the semicolon, see Section 3.3.7.)

SIX TECHNIQUES FOR SUCCESS (Continued)

5. INTERPRET ALL DATA. Technologists rely on visual literacy. A circuit diagram is, after all, one of the best ways for electrical engineers to communicate with one another. However, figures and tables often need verbal explanation in writing, especially if you want your reader to interpret these visuals exactly as you have. Avoid merely referring to graphic aids in your documents; instead, spend some time analyzing those aids so that your reader may follow your presentation and understand your interpretations and conclusions.

6. EMPLOY FREQUENT CLOSURE. In reviewing complex material, readers can often become bogged down. If you fear that your reader may become weary, create closure. Note how the writer in the passage below creates a sense of closure in a lengthy document by summarizing previous material:

> So far in this manual we have provided information on conventional natural gas heating (pp. I 66-67), high efficiency natural gas heating (pp. I 77-81), and electric heating (pp. I 81-87). With this background of heating equipment and systems established, we may now turn to methods of calculating heat loss.

In addition, posing questions and then answering them can be an effective strategy. (See Document 8 in Section 2.4 for an example of this strategy.):

  —What is the significance of these data?
  —What other information is needed?
  —What may be concluded?

Techniques such as these will keep your audience from becoming lost.

CASE STUDY #1:
ANALYZING AN AUDIENCE

You have been asked to prepare an office administration manual for your division. This manual will be used by a broad range of employees—from secretaries to scientists. Included in the manual will be everything from the location of FAX machines to the procedure for submitting an expense report. After thinking about the contents and your audience, use the grid below to identify potential problems in writing a manual for such a diverse audience and to formulate the strategies that you can use to solve these problems.

Component of Manual	Potential Problem	Potential Solution
1.		
2.		
3.		
4.		
5.		

EXERCISE: EVALUATING EFFECTIVE TECHNICAL WRITING

Following are two versions of a sales letter from a commercial sales representative to a potential client. Which version translates the technical material to suit the needs of the reader? Can you identify the strategies of the more effective version?

Version 1

Metroplex Gas Company
P.O. Box 143
South Grange, Indiana   62902

April 29, 19XX

Mr. Christian Gauss
Lakeside Developers
474 Sea Side Heights
South Grange, Indiana   62902

Dear Mr. Gauss:

Subsequent to our conversation last week, I am writing to present further information about the advantage of gas circulating water heating systems.

In your planned 300 unit apartment complex, your initial cost for 720,000 BTU units would be approx. $12,000. In a year, 300 units would use approx. 6.4 Mcf per day at a cost of $5.00. Thus your cost per hour would be about $32.00. If the units operated at 4 hrs./day, that would be $128.00 operating cost a day. At 365 days per year, your cost would be $46,720 per year. In comparison, 300 30 gallon individual water heaters would cost $39,000 initially. These would consume 6817 kwh per unit. If a kwh is $.075, that would be $511.25 per year. Therefore, 300 apartments would cost $153,375. These figures speak for themselves.

If you have any further questions, please feel free to contact me at 523-4435.

Sincerely,

Ray Lynch
Commercial Market Representative

Version 2

Metroplex Gas Company
P.O. Box 143
South Grange, Indiana 62902

April 29, 19XX

Mr. Christian Gauss
Lakeside Developers
474 Sea Side Heights
South Grange, Indiana 62902

Dear Mr. Gauss:

I'm glad we had a chance to talk last week about your planned 300 unit apartment complex on Mulhellen Lane. As promised, I've calculated an approximate estimate of the advantage of gas central water heating.

You'll need four units to make the gas system run efficiently. At a price of $3,000 per unit, the initial cost for the units should run no higher than $12,000. At current gas prices, it would cost $128.00 a day for you to operate the system; the cost of operation for one year would be approximately $46,700.

In comparison, were you to use individual electric water heaters, your initial investment would be approximately $30,000 for 300 heaters with a capacity of 30 gallons each. At current electric prices, it would cost you approximately $153,300 to operate these heaters each year.

What is the gas advantage for you?

—*A savings of nearly $30,000 on the equipment itself,* and

—*A savings of over $106,600 in yearly operational costs.*

In fact, based on the rent you plan to charge, a mere $15.00 added to the rent of each apartment would easily cover your yearly cost of gas to heat the water.

I've worked out these costs in greater detail, and I would welcome the opportunity to go over my calculations with you and your engineers next week. I'll call you in a few days to set up a convenient appointment time. Or, if you'd like, call me at 523-4435.

I look forward to talking with you soon.

Sincerely,

Ray Lynch
Commercial Market Representative

1.3 UNDERSTANDING THE WRITING PROCESS

In 1986, Glenn J. Broadhead and Richard C. Freed investigated the composing process of writers in a business setting. Significant in their findings is the implication that the writing environment defines the writing process. The proposal format specified by a corporation, for instance, often determines how writers plan and organize their documents. Some documents might be revised extensively, while others, written under tight constraints, might not be revised at all. Time, therefore, is an important factor in the composing process.

On the basis of such research the following explains an effective composing process.

This book's discussion of the composing process is based on three stages of classical rhetoric defined by Aristotle; invention (discovering), arrangement (organizing), and style (revising). Rather than prescribe what should occur in each of these stages, questions will be raised that allow you to develop a more effective composing process. As your process improves, so, too, will your technical documents.

Invention

Invention is the initial phase of the composing process. As you explore your ideas, ask yourself the following questions:
—Can I define my reasons for writing this document?
—What information do I need to have before I begin writing in order to achieve accuracy in my document?
—What questions need to be answered in this document?
—What do I know about the needs of my audience?
—Are there any similar documents that will help me develop my new document?

Arrangement

This second stage is the organizational phase of the composing process. As you compose your document, ask yourself these questions:
—When finishing the first paragraph of my document, will my reader know its purpose?
—Is the progress of my ideas easily followed in the document?
—Have I used strong transitions to lead my reader through the document?
—Is there any place in the document where my reader may get lost?
—When completing the document, will my reader have a sense of an ending?

Style

In this final stage the technical writer edits the document. As you put the finishing touches on your document, be sure that you address the following questions:

—Are my sentences brief enough so that my reader will not become tangled in them?

—Is my word choice appropriate to my audience?

—In the tone of my document, have I achieved my intended relationship with my audience?

—Have I defined any technical terms that may confuse my readers?

—Have I checked for lapses in grammar, punctuation, or word choice?

This three-phase description of the composing process will help you submit more effective documents. Remember, though, that these stages overlap. You may stop in the middle of your invention stage in order to check a technical fact, or you may decide to reorganize your document as you revise it for style.

As you perform the various phases of your new composing process, you will become a more effective writer. You will know how to create an engaging lead, to achieve a smooth flow of ideas, and to select concrete words. Remember: the more you practice writing, the more confident you will become.

THE LESSONS OF CLASSICAL RHETORIC ARE IMPORTANT FOR TODAY'S TECHNICAL WRITER

EXERCISE: THINKING ABOUT YOUR WRITING PROCESS

The better you know your own process of composing, the better you will be able to strengthen your most effective strategies. To complete the matrix below, identify three documents you write in your present job. Then, make notes on how you plan, draft, and revise each document.

Kind of document → How do you plan it? → How do you draft it? → How do you revise it?

Type 1: _____

Type 2: _____

Type 3: _____

Now, answer these questions:

1. When you plan each document, how do your processes vary?

   _____

   _____

   _____

2. In your drafting process, are there any strategies that you find especially effective?

   _____

   _____

   _____

3. In your revision process, are there any editing problems that you would like to solve?

   _____

   _____

   _____

1.4 THE FIVE C'S OF REPORT WRITING

To improve the quality of your technical reports, strive to follow *The Five C's of Report Writing*. Make your writing concise, complete, concrete, correct, and coherent.

C NUMBER #1: *Conciseness*

Remember that some words or phrases commonly used are nothing more than excess baggage and consequently may be omitted without any loss of meaning. Instead of writing "in view of the fact that," for example, simply write "because." Strive for terse, lean prose:

Instead of	Use
a large number of	many
through the medium of	by
in the course of	during
in the event of	if
in view of	because

In addition, avoid the frequent use of *-ion* words. This suffix adds length to your words but adds nothing to the meaning of your ideas:

Instead of	Use
altercation	dispute
remuneration	pay
imperfection	fault
admonition	warning

Writers often believe that the *-ion* suffix adds authority to their prose. In reality, these writers fill their writing with stuffy and stilted bureaucratic jargon.

Remember, the more technically complex your information, the more lucid your prose must be. The greatest scientists of this century—Albert Einstein, Robert Oppenheimer, Richard Feynman—all wrote clear, concise prose.

THE FIVE C'S OF REPORT WRITING (Continued)

C NUMBER #2: *Completeness*

A complete document will answer all questions that readers may ask. You must do your job for the reader in order to achieve what writing specialists frequently refer to as reader-based prose.

Imagine the reception a writer would receive if the opening of a memo read as follows:

> A quote has been received, after soliciting various manufacturers a while back, for 100 to 200 units to complete the manufacture of the HVR 200 TAS. For these units, a price was quoted as $473.25 each, plus a one-time installation cost of $7,500.

When were the quotes received? What is the name of the manufacturer? What is the HVR 200 TAS? Who quoted the price of $473.25? Is that the price for each unit or for each set of 100 units? What is being installed for $7,500?

Poor writers will excuse such lack of completeness by claiming that their readers know the situation and will be able to understand the information. This sort of excuse is false for two reasons. First, it assumes that readers who receive scores of documents each day will automatically be able to orient themselves to the case at hand. For the busy reader, time spent trying to recall the details of a memo is time lost. Second, most corporate and government correspondence is public in nature, and so any document potentially has multiple readers. While the intended reader may know the situation described in a document, unintended readers—often those higher in the corporation—will be confused. Note how this confusion is avoided by a revision made with a goal of completeness:

> Last month Fred Markham of Multicycle Systems provided the following quote in response to our need for relay card units. These units will allow circuits on the HRV 200 TAS, our newest satellite, to be assigned randomly in order to minimize blockage and allow uninterrupted transmission. We will need 156 relay card units, each priced at $473.25. In addition, Multicycle engineers will be required to install all 156 units for which there will be a one time charge of $7,500.

As the revision illustrates, in technical writing accuracy and detail are always required.

C NUMBER #3: *Concreteness*

Always avoid expressions that are vague or overworked:

Instead of	*Use*
implement	carry out
utilize	use
prior to	before
terminate	end
optimum	best
facilitate	ease
demonstrate	show

As you revise your documents, ask yourself *exactly* what you mean when you use words such as "appreciable," "considerably," "more or less," or "suitable." What, exactly, do you mean when you say that something is "good" or "bad"? Often, answering these questions will make you fully document the claim that you are making. You may wind up adding sentences and paragraphs to your report in order to clarify your position fully, but your ideas will be clearer both to you and to your readers.

C NUMBER #4: *Correctness*

When writers refer to "correctness," they usually mean the ability to use word choice, grammar, and punctuation according to the conventions of standard English. While we will return to these areas in Section 3, you should know that many writers mistakenly view mere correctness as their only goal in technical writing. Often even professional writers reveal their obsessions with the proper use of the comma or the ways to avoid dangling modifiers.

Yet you are far more than a comma clerk. You already know most of the conventions of standard English. Your goal must now be to move beyond the level of basic literacy and discover how to communicate complex information.

THE FIVE C'S OF REPORT WRITING
(Continued)

C NUMBER #5: *Coherence*

The more technically complex a document, the more likely that your readers will become confused or lost in the detail. Thus your documents must achieve a sense of unity so that your readers will be able to follow the information you present. Use the following three fundamental strategies to make your documents coherent.

Method 1: Transitional Words

The use of key connectors is the most commonly recognized method for achieving unity in a document. Below is a list of some of the most useful transitional words and phrases:

Beginning: first, initially
Continuation: after, as, as soon as, before, during, later, meanwhile, next, second, then, until, upon, when, while
Ending: at last, finally
Classification: can be categorized, can be classified, can be divided
Conclusion: finally, in conclusion
Contrast: although, but, conversely, however, in contrast, on the other hand, whereas, while, yet
Comparison: also, and, as well as, both, in addition, in the same way, like, similarly
Example: an illustration of this, another example of, another illustration of, for example, for instance, to illustrate

Method 2: Repetition of Key Terms

Another method of achieving coherence in a document is to repeat central words or phrases in order to guide your reader. In the paragraph below, note how the highlighted words help the writing to flow:

The electric heat pump *system* is a heater/cooler *system* that pumps heat from one temperature to another by means of a compressor-driven refrigeration cycle. The *system* is made up of an *outdoor unit* and an *indoor unit*. During the winter the *outdoor unit* absorbs heat from the outside air, and the *indoor unit* distributes that heat to the structure being heated. During the summer the *indoor unit* absorbs heat from the structure, and the *outdoor unit* expels the heat. Since the heat pump extracts heat from the outside air, that heat supplements the electricity consumed by the *system*. In fact, a heat pump is capable of producing two to three times as many BTU's of heat per hour as it consumes. It is no wonder that heat pumps are among the most popular energy saving *systems*.

Repetition of key words and phrases lends a sense of unity to what otherwise may have been a confusing explanation.

Method 3: Graphics

The effective use of graphics is one of the most commonly overlooked means of achieving coherence in technical writing. Note the coherence of the following memo:

Date: April 29, 19XX
To: Peter Brierley
From: John Morgan
Subject: Lost SLG Date

A number of operators have complained of lost data since our group switched to the new Multifax system. The two operator actions described below will help prevent loss of SLG data:

1. *Display SLG data collection status regularly.*
2. *Inform Systems Programming immediately if the ACTIVE Dataset reaches 90% at any time.*

1. *Display SLG Date collection status regularly.* First, use the SLG command to produce display number 159. When display 159 is on the screen, one SLG dataset display should show ACTIVE and the other should show ALTERNATIVE. You can then monitor the status of the system.

2. *Inform Systems Programming immediately if the ACTIVE dataset reaches 90% at any time.* If screen 159 is displayed every 30 minutes or so, there is no chance that the system will reach its capacity and therefore lose data.

If these operations are followed, we will decrease our chances of losing SLG data.

Here the writer has used parallel phrases, parallel spacing, and italics to give a sense of unity to the document.

As you study this book, continue to use the 5 C's—**conciseness, completeness, concreteness, correctness, and coherence**—as criteria by which you may evaluate the effectiveness of your own writing. The more aware you are of these essential elements of effective technical writing, the more able you will be to apply them to your own documents.

SECTION 2

DEVELOPING THE
TECHNICAL DOCUMENT

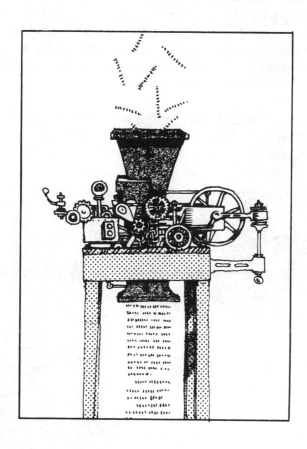

2.0 DEVELOPING THE TECHNICAL DOCUMENT

This section presents various kinds of documents common to the technically oriented workplace. While technical documents vary in their specific design from organization to organization, the kinds of documents we have selected will allow you to understand key structural patterns so that you will be able to tailor those patterns to the kinds of documents you write as part of your job.

How is it possible to find common types of documents in so varied an environment as an organization? Similar kinds of documents may be found because the documents' structural patterns—definition, classification, comparison, contrast—reflect the ways that information is processed within organizations. A new product, for example, must be defined according to its uses, must be classified along with existing products, must be compared and contrasted with its competitors, and must be used according to procedural manuals. Universally, writing is employed to record, to inform, and to argue because the demand for the effective communication is the driving force behind the modern information-based organization.

As you read through Section 2, take careful note of what kind of situation prompts the need for each document and think about how you can adapt your own writing to the document-design strategies that we present.

2.1 CORRESPONDENCE

Communication within organizations is often spoken. We talk to our colleagues in meetings, we gather information by phone, we make technical presentations orally to clients.

This kind of communication, however, is short-lived. In time, the information we receive and provide must be recorded so that it can be used by others. Internally, the memo is used to tell colleagues and employers about our progress on assignments. Externally, letters are used to communicate with others who are not part of our immediate working environment.

2.1.1 The Memo

In field interviews technicians often report that they spend little time composing memos. Although memos are a major part of their writing, the technicians' memos are composed in one draft, checked only for spelling and grammar, and processed for distribution.

Managers, however, tell a different story. They emphasize the importance of well-constructed memos. Some managers' memos on one hand constitute a daily record of an organization's operations and form a permanent record of the status of projects. Since managers frequently take someone's memo and redistribute it to other audiences, in few situations will a writer be sure that a memo will be read only by its intended audience. Practically, this means that the memo must be written so it can be understood by a variety of readers.

On the other hand, some managers use memos as a basis for their own reports for upper management. (In one study the typical manager wrote seven memos a week; in another, managers ranked memos first in frequency among twenty forms of written communication.) If memos are not accurate in detail and lucid in presentation, managers find it impossible to use them to write their own reports. As a consequence, because of poorly written memos, managers will often spend time researching information that should have been presented in memos in the first place. The case is clear: memos must present information lucidly as well as present the background for that information.

CORRESPONDENCE: MEMOS (Continued)

Since memos are the daily operating record of organizations, they are produced in vast quantity. If they are to be read, they must be very well organized to make the information they contain readily apparent. The following are four worthwhile goals for you to pursue in writing a memo. As you study these goals, refer to the model memo provided as Document 1:

1. *Define the purpose within the first two sentences.* Be straightforward in your presentation. Phrases such as ''I am writing to present (or inform or summarize)'' are appreciated by a reader.

2. *Provide enough background so that an unintended reader can understand the information.* Since no one can guarantee that a memo will not be distributed within an organization, it is best to recall briefly the background of the information you present in the memo. Of course, the entire history of a project cannot be retold, yet a sentence or two can set the memo in context so that a reader will have a frame of reference for understanding your information. Note in Document 1, for example, how the writer has included a brief, two-sentence background section so that any reader within her organization will be able to follow her argument to purchase the Smith Water-Waste Filtration System.

3. *Analyze the information you present.* Note how the writer of Document 1 has developed four criteria to analyze the Smith System. These criteria help the reader understand the significance of Ms. Silver's work and the reasons for her conclusion.

4. *Develop a conclusion.* No matter how brief your memo, readers need a sense of an ending. What are they to make of what you have told them? What is significant in the memo? Note that Ms. Silver ends her memo by directly stating that her company should consider the purchase of the XL 3500 Filtration System.

If your memos are to stand out, they must be well crafted. The technical expert who hastily jots down a memo and sends it out is seriously misunderstanding the importance of this kind of document. When you compose your memos, keep the four goals in mind. You will write in a way that is clear to your readers.

DOCUMENT 1: THE MEMO

Date: March 9, 19XX
To: Keith Daniels, VPAA of Systems Development
From: Pam Silver, Field Representative, Division G
Subject: The Smith Water-Waste Filtration System

At your request, last week I met with James Dobson of Smith Corporation regarding their new water-waste filtration system. I am writing to present my analysis of the appropriateness of the Smith XL-3500 Filtration System to our needs here at Cookman's.

Background: As you well know, our Simpson County plant will soon begin operation. Our company's long-standing concern with ecological issues warrants that we look closely at state-of-the-art water waste filtration systems, especially since the Simpson plant will produce over 180 million gallons of contaminated waste-water annually.

Smith Corporation: Smith Corporation, based in Atlanta, Georgia, has been in business for five years. It is well-known in the field of waste-water treatment; in fact, the recent use of a Smith filtration system saved Barney Corporation from a growing reputation as a leading contributor to environmental pollution in our own state.

The Smith Water-Waste Filtration System: The superiority of the Smith System may be judged by five criteria:

1. *Efficiency:* The heart of the Smith system is made of an inert polymer material that can withstand any liquid with a Ph within the range of 0 to 14. The system provides an absolute barrier that prevents all contaminants from being discharged. Materials such as BODs (Biodegradable Organic Ditoxins) and CODs (Concentrated Organic Detergents) are retained almost 99%. The contaminants we will produce at our Simpson County plant—iron, lead, and zinc—are nearly 100% retained.

2. *Compatibility and Future Flexibility:* All Smith systems may easily be tailored to the particular needs of an existing plant. In addition, should any new products or processes alter the characteristics of our plant, Smith can easily accommodate such changes. With this guarantee, there is little chance of the system becoming outdated.

3. *Warranty:* Smith Corporation offers a five-year warranty on all their water-waste filtration systems. The Corporation also guarantees that their system will produce discharged water that is in compliance with all federal, state, and local waste discharge requirements.

4. *Cost:* The Smith system most suited to our needs is the XL-3500 Membrane Filtration System, priced at $145,000. This total price includes a foam control system as well as a computerized chart recorder that will allow us to monitor the system's effectiveness.

5. *Maintenance:* The system membrane is designed to maintain a high rate of productivity along with minimal cleaning requirements. Since the system is made of polypropylene, nylon, stainless steel, and other non-corrosive materials, replacement costs will be minimal. And, since the system's design allows complete contaminant removal with consistenly high filtrate flow rates, a substantial savings in energy costs will be realized.

Conclusion: Judged by these five criteria, the Smith Corporation seems well qualified to provide our new Simpson County plant with the needed water-waste filtration system. Also, recall that the XL-3500 Filtration System is 15% less expensive than that offered by its chief competitor, Metacorp. (See my March 1 memo.) Moreover, since Smith Corporation seems to have excellent upgrade capacity, while Metacorp did not, I believe we should consider further investigation of the Smith XL-3500 Filtration System.

With your permission I would like to set up a meeting with our design team and Mr. Dobson for next week. I look forward to your reply.

CORRESPONDENCE (Continued)

While the memo is the central internal document used in an organization, the central external document is the letter.

While organizations use various types of letters, a common type that is used by individuals to seek career advancement is the cover letter. The cover letter structured according to the plan below serves as a good example of the kind of organizational patterns found in all external correspondence.

Basically, the cover letter of a resume is divided into four sections:

Section 1. Your cover letter should open by mentioning how you came to learn of the position opening, as Craig Bruening has in the first paragraph of Document 2. You should then apply for the position you seek.

Section 2. In this section of your cover letter you should tell your reader about your unique qualifications for the position. Because this information is the most important part of the cover letter, you should spend time designing this section to allow your reader to review your accompanying resume in a way that highlights your unique qualifications for the position. Note that Mr. Bruening has spent two paragraphs developing this section of his letter. He reviews his present duties as they apply to the job he is seeking, and he assures the reader in his next paragraph that he understands the job responsibilities of an environmental field engineer.

Section 3. Introduce any supplementary material that you have for your claim to the position. Obviously a competent writer, Mr. Bruening has decided that his communication skills will give him a competitive edge in his job application. In this section you should also refer to the enclosed resume.

Section 4. In this final section, be direct: ask for an interview and identify when you will be available. Your assertiveness will reflect your interest in pursuing the position. In the closing paragraph of the cover letter, Mr. Bruening says that he will follow up his application with a telephone call.

EXAMPLE

DOCUMENT 2: THE COVER LETTER

1254 King Blvd.
Newark, NJ 07102
June 10, 19XX

Mr. James Fletcher
Operations Manager
TWR Associates
Knoxville, Tennessee 37928

Dear Mr. Fletcher:

On Sunday, October 30, 19XX, I read your advertisement in the <u>New York Times</u> for an environment field engineer. I am writing to apply for that position.

Since my graduation three years ago from the New Jersey Institute of Technology, I have been working as an environmental field engineer for Frank Keller in East Orange, New Jersey. My primary duty has been to design a landfill closure site. As a result, I have had extensive experience with review of landfill closure plans, research sites, and transportation planning. I realize that the position you advertise requires familiarity with ECRA and CERCLA regulations. In my present position I work with these daily. As well, I am familiar with computerized hydrologic modeling.

From your advertisement I asume that the person you seek will be able to supervise the installation of monitoring and production wells on landfills, complete daily soil boring logs, perform on-site chemical analysis of boring samples, and assure site and safety security. I feel that I am qualified to perform these tasks because they are quite similar to many of the responsibilities I held as an engineering technician with Fitzsimmons Corporation. Since I performed many of these duties, I am confident that as a supervisor for TWR Associates, I can assure their successful completion.

My academic background, as my enclosed resume shows, well-prepared me for the position of environmental field engineer. Courses in statistics and hydrology have taught me how to analyze samples taken under a variety of circumstances and to interpret these samples so that management and planning decisions can be made. In addition, my writing skills are quite solid, so I believe that I can serve as a field liaison with your corporate office by producing reports that are accurate and concise.

In a few days' notice I can be available to fly to Knoxville for an interview. Indeed, I plan to be in Memphis for a convention on October 17, so I could easily come to your home office for an interview that week. During the next few days I will call you to see if my credentials fit your company's needs and, if so, when an interview can be arranged. TWR has a superior national reputation, and I would very much like to work for your corporation. Thank you for your consideration. I look forward to talking with you soon.

Sincerely,

Craig Bruening

CORRESPONDENCE (Continued)

2.1.3 The Resume

Accompanying the cover letter is the resume. In combination, they set forth your abilities and talents.

It is often felt that an entire career must be summarized in detail on the resume, but this view is incorrect. Details of your work and educational experiences must be selected with care. Any additional information that is needed to support your application for the job can, after all, be given in the cover letter.

Before writing your resume, you should gather all the information you need about your education and work experiences. Make sure that you include details from your education: your college major, your degree, and your professional certificates or licenses; your knowledge of computers; your proficiency in languages. From your work experience, include these details: your job titles, places of employment, and dates of previous jobs; your job duties, tasks performed, and achievements.

After gathering the above material for your resume, we suggest you use the outline below. As you review the outline, refer to Document 3.

1. *Heading:* Include your name, address, and telephone number. Note that Mr. Bruening has listed both his work and home number.
2. *Career Objective:* Specify the kind of position or field of work in which you are interested.
3. *Work Experience:* List work experience by jobs in reverse chronological order (most recent first). Be sure to highlight your position title. Mr. Bruening has described in detail each of his positions.
4. *Educational Background:* List the colleges you attended and their addresses. Specify your college major and degree. Note that Mr. Bruening has even listed relevant course work.
5. *Miscellaneous Information:* List under defined categories, information on academic honors, professional memberships, licenses, certifications, language proficiency, and computer proficiency.

Do not include the following: a photo of yourself, your sex and age, your political and religious affiliations, or your salary expectations.

Use the following list of action verbs to help make your work experiences come alive:
administered, analyzed, approved, arranged, conceived, conducted, contracted, controlled, coordinated, created, designed, developed, directed, enlarged, established, examined, expanded, guided, implemented, improved, invented, investigated, managed, organized, planned, presented, recruited, researched, reshaped, revised, scheduled, strengthened, supervised, trained, wrote.

A final word. Most companies prefer a brief but complete one or two-page resume and expect it to be expertly edited. A sloppy, untidy resume will suggest that you may have little interest or motivation in the position. Consequently, spend time preparing your resume so that it serves as your professional introduction to a prospective employer.

Document 3: THE RESUME

Craig T. Bruening

1254 King Blvd.   (201) 828-5642 (Work)
Newark, NJ   07102   (201) 678-4443 (Home)

CAREER OBJECTIVE

Hazardous and toxic waste investigation.

PROFESSIONAL EXPERIENCE

Environmental Engineer
May 19XX-Present
Frank Keller & Associates, East Orange, NJ
> Designed landfill closure plan for a superfund site; performed review of landfill closure plans; researched potential ECRA and CERCLA sites and managed roadway and utility access design for the East Ferry Resource Recovery Facility.

Environmental Engineering Technician
June 19XX-May 19XX
Fitzsimmons Corporation, Parsippany, NJ
> Installed wells on landfills; completed daily soil boring samples; enforced company safety plan.

Financial Systems Analyst
October 19XX-June 19XX
Citgo Central Services, Florham Park, NJ
> Planned financial operations for Citgo's Education Center; managed operations budget of 4.1 million dollars; created computerized billing procedure; trained Education Center staff.

EDUCATION

New Jersey Institute of Technology, Newark, NJ.
19XX-19XX   GPA: 3.5/4.0
Major: BSCE   Minor: Technical Communications

Course work included: statistics, surveying, strength of materials, fluid mechanics, elementary structures, transportation, water resources, and technical writing.

West Virginia University, Morgantown, W. VA
19XX-19XX   GPA: 3.7/4.0
Major: A.S. in Engineering Technology
Course work included: structural geology, stratification and sedimentation, and mineralogy.

ACADEMIC HONORS

Member, Chi Epsilon, The National Civil Engineering Society
Member, Tau Beta Pi, The National Engineering Honor Society
Co-Op Scholar in Civil Engineering

REFERENCES

Available Upon Request

2.2 REPORTS

While the memo is the most common type of internal document, often its brief form proves insufficient. More detailed documents—reports—are then required.

There are many types of reports. Here are models of two of the most common: the trip report and the monthly report.

2.2.1 The Trip Report

You are sent on business trips to act on behalf of your organizations. While you may informally present in a staff meeting, information you gathered during the trip, a formal document is required so that the information may be preserved for study by others.

A well-designed trip report will answer the following questions:

1. *What was the extent and nature of your trip?* Briefly describe the details of the trip; especially include those individuals who were important in the situation. (Make sure that names are spelled correctly and that titles are accurate.)
2. *What were the most important aspects of your trip?* Do not narrate the events of the trip. Instead, classify the major events of the trip so that your reader can see that you analyzed the information you obtained.
3. *What conclusions did you reach?* Implicitly, we are sent on trips to gather information, sort it out, and report on its significance. Hence, trip reports are sometimes written to persuade as well as to inform. In the final section of your report you might wish to point out any areas of importance that may be significant to your readers.

Document 4 represents a model trip report. We feel that it is excellent for the following reasons:

—*The writer clearly establishes the context of the report.* Since Megatech's president and vice president of engineering were present, the reader realizes that the meeting was significant.

—*The writer identifies the most important aspects of the trip.* Instead of a long narrative, the writer focuses on the visit to Megatech's production and installation capabilities, the analysis of the assembly and systems test, and the review of the quality assurance program.

—*The writer uses an engaging lead and organizes the report around the lead.* In the first sentence the reader is told the three reasons for the trip. The report is then organized around these three sections. Note that parallel word choice between the lead and the sections helps to keep the reader on track. (Recall the discussion of coherence in Section 1.4.)

—*The writer helps the reader analyze the situation.* Note, however, that the writer does not suggest that his company sign Megatech onto the project. Such a suggestion would not be appropriate because the writer was asked only to review and to report on an assembly procedure, not to make a recommendation. The writer simply says that "Megatech could equip its facility to meet the demand." This kind of analysis enables the reader to add the writer's analysis to the existing information and to make a sharper management decision.

DOCUMENT 4: THE TRIP REPORT

Communicom Interoffice Report #23

To: Mark Lawrence   Mail Drop: 1-23   Date: 11/23/XX

From: Huan Phen   Mail Drop: 1-27   Telephone: 5562

Subject: Trip Report: Review of Megatech Facility

On November 21, P. Merts, L. Patel, and I returned from a review of Megatech Corporation's Antenna Assembly Facility in Santa Clara, California, to determine Megatech's production capabilities for assembly of the 2.7 meter antenna, to view the antenna assembly, and to investigate Megatech's quality assurance program.

Present at the meetings were the following representatives from Communicom and Megatech:

Communicom:

H. Phen: Electrical Engineering
P. Merta: Mechanical Engineering
L. Patel: Manufacturing

Megatech:

L. Perez: President
R. Cohn: VP, Engineering
R. Smith: Plant Manager

Production Capabilities

For over six years Megatech Corporation has been manufacturing 2.7 meter antenna systems and has installed over 250 systems throughout the United States and Mexico. Occupying a 27,000 square foot warehouse, Megatech has a staff of 15 full-time employees, most of whom are electrical and mechanical engineers with specializations in engineering technology.

Currently, Megatech is able to manufacture 5 antenna systems per week. However, if awarded our contract, the President and Vice President of engineering indicated that they would be willing to purchase 7 additional antenna molds and hire 5 additional technicians. The plant would then be able to increase its weekly manufacturing capacity to 10 antenna systems per week. Recall that over the next two years we will need approximately 500 antenna systems. Megatech believes that their technicians could easily handle our project.

Page 1 of 2

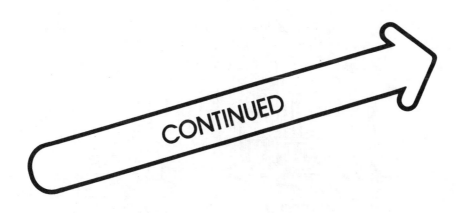

CONTINUED

DOCUMENT 4: THE TRIP REPORT (Continued)

Antenna Assembly

P. Martz, L. Patel, and I watched as an antenna was assembled. It took two technicians approximately 1.5 hours to assemble an antenna. The work, we agreed, was performed efficiently and effectively by technicians who are obviously experienced and comfortable with the procedure.

We were especially impressed when an LNA test was being performed and the antenna under assembly failed. The two assembly technicians called over another technician who was a designated LNA test troubleshooter. The two technicians then began work on another antenna. Within 45 minutes the troubleshooter solved the problem on the original antenna, and the new antenna had been assembled. This sort of planning and efficiency in Megatech's plant indicates a sophisticated operation.

Quality Assurance

Although L. Patel is preparing the comprehensive report on QA, it is clear that the testing procedure for the antenna was thorough. R. Smith produced documentation that there has been a complaint rate of less than 2% on the 2.7 meter antenna, and these problems were easily resolved by a Megatech representative.

Conclusion

P. Mertz, L. Patel, and I believe that Megatech could equip its facility to meet the demand for providing the antenna systems that we will need next year.

However, if a greater number of systems were required in a shorter time, a case indicated in L. Filmore's Interoffice Report #19, then we do not believe that Megatech could equip its facility to meet the demand. The plant technicians are highly qualified and well trained, but hiring and training new technicians in a short time period would be a problem for so small a corporation.

If any additional information is needed, please let me know.

Page 2 of 2

WELCOME TO MEGATECH

2.2.2 *The Activities Report*

Organizations ask their employees to report on their activities. Whether submitted weekly or monthly, these reports provide updated information on projects.

Often, however, activities reports are neglected documents, dashed off the morning they are due for submission. This strategy is ill advised for two reasons. First, as in the case of memos, managers communicate with one another by means of activities reports: managers tell us that they draw upon items from activities reports to write their own reports. As we have seen many times, an especially well-written item could be distributed by your group manager and eventually wind up on the desk of the CEO. Second, these reports are a chance to let management know about your efforts. Both problems and successes may be recorded formally in these reports and thus promote action and praise for your work.

When planning your activities report, be sure to review the following questions:

1. *How can I best illustrate the significance of my work?* Since your readers will not want a minute-by-minute explanation of your activities, you should provide a summary of your most important activities and their relevance. Careful selection, not exhaustive detail, is what is needed.

2. *Are there any activities that require updating?* All projects are organic in nature, and so they shift as they develop. As situations evolve, be sure that your readers are informed of any changes that may alter the progress of the projects.

3. *Are there any new projects that you have begun?* Often your company or a client will ask you to take on new responsibilities. Be sure to recall the significance of these projects for your readers.

4. *Are there any special efforts you have made during the reporting period?* Opportunities often arise by which project goals may be quickly reached. If you have focused especially on one project, be sure to review these activities for your readers.

5. *Are there any activities outside of the workplace which may be of interest?* Association meetings, community involvement, continuing education—all are important to your career development. If you are participating in any extended project that may help you reach a specified project goal, make sure to mention it in your report.

THE ACTIVITIES REPORT (Continued)

After considering questions such as those listed on page 35, you will want to write an activities report that will be read with interest, not skimmed in haste. Below are the criteria for writing a successful activities report:

1. *Define all activities fully.* Do not assume that your reader can identify all the names, dates, and places you refer to in your report. Instead of writing that you "picked up a letter of credit from James Frank for the condo development," you should write that you "picked up a letter of credit on June 3 from James Frank of the Colorado Land Corporation for the condominiums to be developed by Boulder Industries."

2. *Avoid abbreviations.* A manager who has to read twenty or so activity reports can become confused by the hundreds of abbreviations used in an organization. While some generic abbreviations are easily recognizable (PC for "personal computer"), other technical ones may be confusing (COP for "coefficient of performance").

3. *Select strong verbs.* Verbs such as *did, get, saw,* or *went* are characteristically weak verbs. *Installed, purchased, reviewed,* or *traveled* are much more specific verbs that describe more fully your activities.

4. *Keep these verbs parallel in structure.* After selecting verbs, make sure that they are grammatically consistent. Note in Document 5 that the writer's verbs are all consistently in the past tense: *reviewed, outlined,* and *installed.*

5. *Be brief.* As shown in Document 5, individual items in activities reports should be concise. Well-constructed entries of one or two lines are preferable to rambling paragraphs.

AVOID FLOWERY LANGUAGE

DOCUMENT 5: THE ACTIVITIES REPORT

June 5, 19XX through June 10, 19XX
Ruth Davis
Level 2 Specialist
Computer Services Group

ACTIVITIES REPORT

Project C41765: Systems Development Support

Administrative Services
Reviewed PL1 programs with Ilish Soliven (Director of Administrative Services). Design problems with the program suggest that review is needed. The problems can be resolved in 3 or 4 hours next week.

Project C41776: User Support

Safety Department
Met with James Stephens (Level 2 Engineer) to help him define his stylesheet needs. Since Management Planner will be the most help to him, I loaded the system on his PC.

Market Research
Reviewed Market Research Director Erik Parish's report on reconciliation problems between XV3200 Data Base and the hand tallied weekly tickets. This problem seems major, so I have called a meeting for June 12 at 10:00 a.m. in Conference Room B with Madeline Sylvester, our Market Research Specialist.

Project 41767: Micro Support

Legal Department
Installed LOTUS and updated Word Planner from series 4.0 to series 5.0 on the 5 ATs in the Legal Division.

Information Center
—Installed modems on Information Center's Model 80 terminal.
—Assisted Mark Summer (Information Agent) in setting the margins on Word Planner so that it would print according to the new document design specifications from Document Services.

Project 41769: Document Services

Training
Conducted 3 half-day classes on Hyper Graphics for the writers. Skills assessment taken on the last day of class indicated that all participants have achieved 90% mastery of the program.

Miscellaneous

—Attended meeting at our Cincinnati plant on new spreadsheet applications.
—Registered for course in Advanced Computer Applications in the evening division at Urbana County College.

2.3 PROPOSALS

Proposals are argumentative in nature. Designed to persuade a defined audience, they are written to present a unique plan of action.

Generally, proposals may be classified as internal or external. While an internal proposal is written for use within an organization, an external proposal is aimed at an audience outside of the organization. Internally, for example, you might propose a fresh way of looking at a nagging company problem; externally, you might be part of a team answering a call for proposals from a government agency.

Proposals may be brief or extended. Often, as is illustrated in Document 6, a brief proposal takes the form of a letter. On the other hand, an external proposal, as shown in Document 7, may take the form of a report.

However, it is not helpful to think of proposals as informal (haphazard) or formal (lifeless). Regardless of the relationship between writer and audience, proposals must be carefully structured to advance your plan of action.

On pages 39–45, there are the argumentative strategies taken by two writers involved in different situations.

2.3.1 The Brief Proposal

In Document 6, Charles Macklin, a market specialist for a large gas company, must persuade Reverend Kenneth Majors, pastor of a rural church, to consider adopting natural gas as a heating source. While Macklin realizes that he must argue the advantages of natural gas over butane as an energy source, he also realizes that he must translate the complex calculations used to determine cost savings so that they are clear to a non-specialist. (Recall Figure 2). Additionally, Macklin realizes that he must present his reader with the potentially upsetting fact that laying a main line extension to the church will be costly.

Careful study of Document 6 reveals that Macklin has woven a tight argument:

In the opening paragraph, he recalls his previous meeting with Reverend Majors and establishes the aim of the letter: that a natural gas energy source will afford a cost savings.

In the second paragraph, Macklin makes some clever translation decisions. He gives just enough information so that the non-specialist reader will be able to understand the basis of the calculations, but he does not provide the detailed calculations themselves. Further, he translates the significance of calculations: over a 10-year period, the church would save over $12,790 by using natural gas instead of butane. Note that Macklin uses underlining to emphasize this most important information. (Recall the discussion of graphics in Section 1.4.)

In the third paragraph, Macklin breaks the bad news: the cost of extending a line to the church would be approximately $10,000. Note that Macklin does not try to hide this fact, nor bury it within another paragraph. The information is presented in a straightforward, ethical manner.

In the fourth paragraph, Macklin presents a counter argument to the potential problem presented in the third paragraph. He estimates the rate of return credit that the church will receive, and he reminds the Reverend that all future buildings will benefit from the cost savings afforded by natural gas.

In the closing paragraph, Macklin is persuasive. While friendly in tone, he alerts his reader that he will call early the next week to discuss further the advantages of natural gas.

In essence, Macklin's letter is an excellent model of a brief proposal. He advances his company's position in a document that is argumentative in nature. With the benefits clearly and fairly presented, he can then further promote his company's product.

DOCUMENT 6: THE BRIEF PROPOSAL

Twin Cities Gas Corporation
346 Main Street
Fort Worth, Texas   75051

Jan. 22 19XX

Reverend Kenneth Majors
Maplevale Church
Grandview, Texas   75428

Dear Reverend Majors:

It was my pleasure to talk to you last week regarding the planned renovation of your church's heating system. I am writing to give you the estimated savings you will realize if you select a natural gas heating system.

Using your present heating source, butane, you paid $3021 during the year 1989-1990. Using $.78/gal (our regional price), I was able to calculate your butane consumption during this period. Had you used natural gas (at the regional price of $.0055/cf) during this same period, the cost of heating your church would have been $1742. Thus, your parish would have saved $1279. Over a ten-year period, you would save over $12,790 by using natural gas instead of your present energy source.

In order to supply gas to the church, a main line extension of approximately 1,000 feet will be required. Since the nearest gas line is located on North Main Street, the cost of extending this line to the church would be approximately $10,000.

However, for each $100 of natural gas consumed during the first year, Twin Cities Gas Corporation will refund the parish $300 toward the cost of the extension. Since the church will use approximately $1742 of natural gas in a one-year period, I estimate that you will regain the cost of your deposit in two and one half years. In addition, the new school you are planning would receive the advantage of natural gas heating without the cost of an extension because you would already be providing for the future by your current investment.

We at Twin Cities believe we can offer your congregation a substantial energy savings. I'll call you early next week to see if you will need any further information. In the meantime, if you have any questions, please contact me at 214-886-5412, ext. 45.

Yours,

Charles Macklin
Market Specialist

2.3.2 The Extended Proposal

Complex situations often require a very sophisticated presentation, as Jim Gentlin apparently knows. A lab technician, he addresses a nagging company problem and resolves it elegantly. To argue his point, he follows a complex argumentative pattern which deserves our attention.

The proposal in Document 7 is effective because it is integrated into distinct sections, each advancing Jim's argument a step at a time:

Part I: *The Lead.* Jim defines the context of the proposal by answering questions of who, when, why, where, and how. After briefly defining the problem—Row corporation has been having trouble with the airflow controller—Jim "telegraphs" to his reader the plan his proposal will follow: a discussion of the Uniflow 310's compatibility, reliability, cost, and warranty.

Part II: *The Current Environment.* Many times proposals fail because their context is not established for the reader. In identifying component and assembly problems with the Magna 51Z, Jim pinpoints the kinds of problems that have resulted from use of antiquated equipment. By analyzing problems and not merely complaining about them, Jim sets the stage for introducing his proposal.

Part III: *Gains:* Jim moves into the heart of his proposal. By following the plan set forth in the lead, he continues his categorical argument. The Uniflow 310 should be purchased, Jim argues, because of its compatibility, reliability, warranty, and cost.

In presenting his argument in this manner, Jim anticipates questions that the reader would have about the new airflow controller: Is it compatible with the Row blowers? If so, is the Uniflow 310 reliable? Does it have a solid warranty? How much will the Uniflow cost? In structuring his proposal to answer technical as well as financial questions, Jim strengthens the persuasiveness of his proposal.

THE EXTENDED PROPOSAL (Continued)

Note also that Jim follows a three-step plan for integrating tables into a text. First, he presents tables in the body of the proposal, not stuck away in an appendix where they will be neglected. Second, Jim labels and titles his tables and presents data that are easy to follow. Third, and most important, Jim analayzes the data for his reader. Because it is a mistake to believe that readers will interpret information in the same way as writers do, Jim leads his audience to the inevitable conclusion that the Uniflow 51Z is compatible with the Row blowers. Since the Uniflow 310 performs as well as the Magna 51Z, it may also be inferred that this new airflow controller will serve the company faithfully for the next 20 years.

Part IV: *Possible Problems.* Successful writers always try to identify and address the potential disadvantages of their proposals. If a reader's possible objections can be anticipated and answered within the document, the argument has a far better chance for success. Jim calls attention to possible training problems, but he makes it clear that such problems are not insurmountable.

Part V: *Solutions.* Training, Jim argues, will not in fact be a problem for the technicians. Significantly, in Sections IV and V, Jim performs one of the subtlest of all proposal strategies: he has refuted a weakness in his own proposal; he thus cements the logic of his plan for his reader.

Part VI: *Alternatives.* In a few sentences Jim shows that there are no realistic alternatives to his proposal. Now, he argues, is the proper time to make the transition to the Uniflow 310.

Part VII: *Summary.* By briefly summarizing the structure of his proposal, Jim allows his reader to feel the strength of his argument. As a result of this strategy, the last passage that Juanita Estifan reads emphasizes the point that the Uniflow 310 is the right airflow controller for the Row corporation.

Clearly, in this proposal the writer has completed his task well and led the reader to realize the feasibility of the plan. The rigorous structure presented in Document 7 is found in many of the best proposals. We highly recommend its structure as a model for extended proposals.

DOCUMENT 7: THE EXTENDED PROPOSAL

Date: October 17, 19XX
To: Juanita Estifan, Vice President
From: Jim Gentlin, Lab Technician
Subject: Proposal to Purchase Uniflow 310 Airflow Controller

Here at Row Corporation, we have used the same airflow controller—the Magna 51Z—for the past twenty years. The controller performed faithfully until the summer of 19XX when a shipment of over 200 circuit boards were returned to our supplier for an inability to calibrate. Significantly, the situation reminded us of the potential problems which await us because of the Magna 51Z's outdated technology.

A more modern controller—the Uniflow 310—should be substituted for our own on the basis of its compatibility, reliability, cost, and warranty.

CURRENT ENVIRONMENT

Two current problems reveal the need to replace the Magna 51Z with the Uniflow 310 air controller.

Component Problems

In June 19XX, a shipment of airflow controller boards was returned to Lehigh Electronics, our supplier, because our quality control department could not calibrate the boards. It was suspected that an altered trimmer potentiometer value was the problem. Lehigh was obliged to return the boards with corrected values; however, when we retested them, they still failed to calibrate properly. After some testing it was concluded that a faulty UJT (unijunction transistor) made by Motorsound was the problem. In a meeting with Motorsound engineers and quality control technicians, we were told that, although the UJT on our present order would be replaced, the airflow controller model Magna 51Z was about to be phased out due to a lack of demand. It was clear that the Motorsound's remaining stock would soon be depleted.

Assembly Problem

After Magna 51Z controller boards are shipped to us, wires are soldered to the boards, and they are mounted into a case. Each of these steps takes a great deal of time; the mounting, for instance, requires the time-consuming installation of five small spaces located between the case and the triac.

GAINS

The superiority of the Uniflow 310 may be established through an examination of four criteria.

Compatibility

Before any replacement decisions can be considered, compatibility must be established between the Magna 51Z, the Uniflow 310, and our Row blowers. Therefore, the two airflow controllers were tested with the following blowers: 2EB2500, 2EB412, 2EB512, and 2NB612. These units were chosen because of the great production volume they must handle. The tests were run with the motor voltage monitored and input voltage held constant while the temperature probe was placed in a bath of water at the noted temperature. These temperatures—80 and 90 degrees—are the specification points for minimum and maximum airflow. Table 1 on the next page summarizes the test results.

THE EXTENDED PROPOSAL (Continued)

Table 1. Comatibility Tests Between the Row Blowers, the Magna 51Z, and the Uniflow 310

Unit Model	Controller	Probe Temp.	Motor Voltage
2EB2500	Magna 51Z	80 degrees	38.3
2EB2500	Uniflow 310	80 degrees	35.6
2EB2500	Magna 51Z	90 degrees	105.0
2EB2500	Uniflow 310	90 degrees	110.1
2EB412	Magna 51Z	80 degrees	38.3
2EB412	Uniflow 310	80 degrees	36.0
2EB412	Magna 51Z	90 degrees	105.0
2EB412	Uniflow 310	90 degrees	109.9
2EB512	Magna 51Z	80 degrees	38.3
2EB512	Uniflow 310	80 degrees	38.0
2EB512	Magna 51Z	90 degrees	105.0
2EB512	Uniflow 310	90 degrees	109.1
2NB612	Magna 51Z	80 degrees	38.3
2NB612	Uniflow 310	80 degrees	37.5
2NB612	Magna 51Z	90 degrees	105.0
2NB612	Uniflow 310	90 degrees	109.8

As Table 1 clearly indicates, the Uniflow 310 is capable of operating just like our present controller, the Magna 31Z. Additionally, the Uniflow 310 seems to react faster to changes in temperature, but this impression needs to be documented.

Reliability

I spoke with the Uniflow sales representative, Margaret Lewis, who told me that no major failures were reported on the 310, the unit under review. Other vendors who use the Uniflow 310 include Delta Electric and Universal Industries.

Cost

Tables 2 and 3 illustrate a comparison between the cost of the Magna 51Z and the Uniflow 310:

Table 2. Cost of the Magna 51Z

Printed Circuit Board:	$5.12
Case:	$4.85
Components:	$16.35
Probe:	$5.85
Labor:	$16.87
TOTAL COST/UNIT	$49.05

Table 3. Cost of the Uniflow 310

Printed Circuit Board:	$5.17
Case:	$4.32
Components:	$9.00
Probe:	$3.72
Labor:	$9.89
TOTAL COST/UNIT	$32.10

The Uniflow 310 is less expensive than the Magna 51Z by $16.95. Since we will have to purchase at least 100 units, our savings would be approximately $1,695.00.

Warranty

Although the Magna 51Z has only a six-month manufacturer's warranty, the Uniflow 310 has a one-year warranty on all parts.

POSSIBLE PROBLEMS

The greatest obstacle to the adoption of the Uniflow 310 is the matter of training for initial installation: the assembly department must be taught how to use the new connectors and tools used on a Uniflow 310.

SOLUTIONS

Tooling of the connectors is very similar to other tasks performed by our assembly technicians. Only a few hours should be needed to teach the entire department how to use the tools.

ALTERNATIVES

Soon, Motorsound will phase out the Magna 51Z. Once this occurs, we will be forced to purchase another airflow controller. Since our clients seem to be increasing, we must keep up with manufacturing demands; therefore, this is as good a time as any to make the transition to Uniflow.

SUMMARY

Since a new brand of airflow controller will soon be needed for our plant, the Uniflow 310 seems a solid investment because of its compatibility, reliability, cost, and warranty. The only possible problem—training—will easily be resolved by our expert technicians. Since we can make the transition to the Uniflow 310 now for a little less than the cost of a small personal computer, now is the time to purchase 100 units of the Uniflow 310 airflow controller.

CASE STUDY #2:
THINKING ARGUMENTATIVELY

Frank Stiller is a senior lab technician in a medium-sized company that designs air conditioning units. He believes that his lab, as it is currently set up, is insufficient for the volume of work which must be handled there.

There are two sets of holding shelves capable of storing only 24 air conditioners. However, on the average 50 to 100 air conditioners are in the lab because the company has greatly increased in business. As a result, air conditioners are scattered on the floor, a situation which delays the testing process when a unit must be located.

Write a memo in which Frank proposes to his supervisor, George Victor, that additional racks should be purchased for the lab.

(The analysis of how the proposal might be structured on page 48.)

Continue your memo below:

AUTHORS' RESPONSE THIS WAY

AUTHORS' ANALYSIS OF CASE STUDY #2

Franks' proposal should be structured as follows:

Heading: Frank's proposal should take the form of an extended proposal written in a memo format. The date, writer, reader, and subject should be established in the heading.

Lead: This introduction to the document should be very brief and specific, perhaps no more than three sentences. Frank should establish the reason why he is writing and the gains that will be realized by the adoption of his plan.

Current Environment: Frank might recall the details of the present lab design: the demands placed on the technicians, the inefficiency of the present situation, the results of that inadequacy. The current situation is perhaps so poor that technicians cannot complete their work during the normal business day and so overtime is paid. A thoughtful analysis of the current situation will prepare Frank's audience to be receptive to his ideas.

Gains: Frank should now provide the major thrust of his proposal by presenting the benefits of adding additional racks to the lab. Gains such as efficiency, organization, and savings might be identified as three major benefits to the company.

Possible Problems: Frank might identify at least three possible problems in his proposal. First, there may be a work slowdown while shelves are installed. Second, a reliable supplier of the racks must be found; perhaps a number of suppliers might have to submit bids. Third, because the purchase of the racks would not directly lead to improved production, an investment in the lab might not be viewed by management as a primary concern.

Solutions: Now that Frank has acknowledged potential obstacles, he can refute them. First, he might design a plan in which a contractor could be hired to start the installation on a Friday, work through the weekend, and complete the job on Sunday. Work in the lab would then be slowed down for only one day. Second, with some research Frank might contact the supplier of the original racks to inquire about cost and warranty. Or, perhaps another division in the company—the warehouse?—has installed racks recently; if so, a supplier might be found there. Regarding the issue of cost, Frank must convince management that the time the technicians will save and the improved appearance of the lab will outweigh the cost of the shelves. In addition, the early stages of research and development, in which the lab plays an important role, would be completed more efficiently with the new lab design.

Alternatives: Admittedly, Frank might be able to find few alternatives to the redesign of the lab and the addition of shelves. Adding technicians, for example, would obviously only be a short-term solution. Therefore, Frank might use this section to reiterate his point: if the company is to stay ahead of the competition in research and design, then the lab needs additional shelves.

Cost: To a manager, this item is perhaps the most significant section of the report. Frank should have contacted two or more suppliers before writing the report, gathered information, and obtained bids. This information should be presented in tabular form. In addition, a comparison should be made between the cost of the shelves and the cost of overtime. For example, if the company is spending $15,000 a year on overtime, this cost can be easily eliminated with the purchase of the new shelves.

Summary: In a final paragraph Frank should review the major ideas of his proposal. He should stress the gains in efficiency, organization, and savings. He should cite briefly the obstacles and then show how each might be resolved. The entire cost should be re-stated, and the proposal should end with a well-phrased statement of conviction.

Before submitting his proposal, Frank should have a co-worker read over his proposal and respond to questions such as these:

1. Is my aim in writing this proposal immediately clear?

2. Do I categorically analyze the current environment, or do I merely seem to narrate the problem?

3. Have I selected well-defined, appealing gains for our company?

4. Have I anticipated the kinds of possible problems management might have with this proposal? Have I refuted these possible problems convincingly?

5. Is my alternative the most appealing solution?

6. Are my data well presented in the cost section? Are there any questions about cost which I have not anticipated?

7. After you read the last paragraph, do you feel inclined to accept my proposal?

8. Have I chosen the best typeface, line spacing, and headings for the proposal? Is anything in page design distracting?

9. Are there any distracting errors in grammar, mechanics, or word choice?

If Frank follows this plan, he will write a 5 to 6-page proposal that will be difficult to reject.

2.4 PROCEDURES

When instructions are needed, procedural documents are created. Whether you provide a one-page set of instructions on how to fill out a dental form or a complex manual on how to manipulate a software program, all effective procedures share four design elements:

1. *Attention to audience.* Instructional documents begin with the intended audience. Will the audience be specialists familiar with the language of the procedure? Or will the audience be non-specialists requiring more explanation and definition of terms? Will the audience be hostile, indifferent, or receptive to the procedure? What will be the best tone for you to employ? Such questions answered at the invention stage of the writing process will enable you to make initial planning decisions before writing the text.

Note, for instance, how the author of Document 8 uses an informal question and answer format. Because he realizes that many first-time computer users are fearful of the technology, he establishes his helpful role through using this non-threatening format.

2. *Attention to carefully selected steps.* What are the major steps of the procedure? What are the sub-steps? What steps produce results outside of the task at hand? At what point in the process are readers likely to become confused?

3. *Attention to effective design elements.* Often, we speak of user friendly documents as if this quality were achieved by magic. In fact, a reader-centered document is produced when graphic elements complement verbal elements. Typography, line spacing, levels of headings, insertion of diagrams—all must be considered if an effective procedure is to be written. In Document 8, for example, the writer has identified three steps, listed them, underlined them for emphasis, and selected precise verbs for each action: "contact," "present," and "coordinate."

4. *Attention to field testing.* Before it is put in final form, the procedural document should be reviewed by members of the target audience. After the draft document is tested, the writer should interview the intended audience by asking the following questions:

   —When you are following the procedure, is there any place that you become lost or confused?
   —Are the steps and sub-steps presented logically?
   —Do you feel confident that the procedure can be used by others with your background?

Testing the effectiveness of the document is a step essential to completing all effective documents to make sure that they can do the job for which they were designed.

DOCUMENT 8: THE PROCEDURAL DOCUMENT

Date: February 19, 19XX
To: All Members of Group G
From: Abraham Levison, Systems Development
Subject: Purchase of Personal Computers

What is the purpose of this guide?

During the past year many members of Group G have found it helpful to use personal computers (PCs) in their work. Since we are currently purchasing a good deal of hardware and software, now is an excellent time to coordinate our efforts. This brief procedural guide is written for those planning to purchase a PC.

How do I know if I need a PC?

The personal business computer should be purchased if you are involved in any of these activities:

—Support tasks with work involving group members

—Repetitive operations requiring great accuracy

—Maintenance of small data files

—Access to computerized data bases of vendors

—Data manipulation to develop projections and analyze alternatives, and/or

—Generation of documents that demand professional appearance.

What is the procedure for purchasing a PC?

The three steps in purchasing a PC are as follows:

   Step 1. <u>Contact the Office of the Director, Systems Development Department, to discuss your needs.</u> The Systems Development Department is very knowledgeable about personal computers, word processors, hardware, and software and so will provide invaluable assistance in determining the best purchase at the best possible cost.

   Step 2. <u>Present a written proposal and a purchase request (Form 2440A) for approval.</u> The proposal must be divided into 3 sections. Section I must establish the need for a PC and analyze the benefits resulting from a PC purchase. Section II must identify the specific purchase(s) in mind. Section III must include an itemized statement of cost for all proposed hardware and software purchases.

   Step 3. <u>Coordinate all future purchases with Systems Development.</u> After your PC and its software arrive, be sure to continue to coordinate all your purchases through Systems Development so that compatibility may be maintained throughout the group and so that a library of resources may be developed.

If these steps are followed, Group G will benefit from a coordinated purchase effort.

If you have any questions, don't hesitate to call me at X3266.

2.5 LONG DOCUMENTS

So far we have discussed documents of only a few pages. Many documents, however, are extensive, often running hundreds of pages. Requests for proposals, user's manuals, long-term planning reports may all be quite long.

The following general format is often used for long documents:

Letter of Transmittal: Unattached to the main document, the letter of transmittal may be either a memo (for internal correspondence) or a letter (for external correspondence). It should open with a reference to the enclosed long document and may summarize in a few sentences the contents and the significance of that document. In Document 9, the writer has elected to do both.

Title Page. This page contains the title of the document, its date of submission, its writer, and its audience. Document 10 presents a model.

Abstract. This one- or two-page self-sufficient summary is, in essence, the document in miniature. Since some readers may read only this section, it is important that the abstract be accurate and present the document in the best possible light. As is evident in Document 11, the body and the major points of a long document may be summarized on one page.

Table of Contents. The table of contents allows the reader to gain an accurate overview of the report. In Document 12, for example, the table of contents reflects the argument itself for the need to establish documentation procedures. Also note that the pages are numbered by section so that the manual can be updated without reprinting the entire document.

List of Figures: Including all figures, tables, graphs, charts, and illustrations, this addition to the table of contents allows readers a quick reference to visual information contained in the document. Document 13 provides a List of Figures.

Body. Varying according to situations and specifications, the body of the document usually contains an introductory section, a central section, and a concluding section.

Appendix. Supplementary tables and figures are provided in the appendix. However, it is best to include all significant graphically displayed information within the body of the document so that the audience while reading will be able to refer to the information.

Remember that writing a long document is a complex process involving extensive planning before the project is begun. We recall numerous cases where a document that took months to produce failed miserably because initial planning decisions were not made. The ideal team of writers and editors includes representatives of the groups who will be affected by the document. An office administration manual, for instance, should be written and edited by an internal team composed of clerical staff and management and not by an external consultant. Early decisions on who is best to write and to edit a lengthy document will result in success.

Long documents take time to compose and are expensive to produce. Our experience has shown that the cost of publication usually far exceeds the cost of composition. Binders, division tabs, and reproduction can easily run into thousands of dollars. If the document is to be brought in under budget, planning decisions on publication must be made before the composing process is begun.

DOCUMENT 9: LETTER OF TRANSMITTAL

Central Wyoming Bank
245 Maplevale Drive
Laramie, Wyoming 53404
307-242-7658

Internal Memorandum

Date: December 23, 19XX
To: Andrew Zelhart, Vice President for Operations
From: August Plata, Document Design Manager
Subject: *Document Standards Manual*

Enclosed is the new *Document Standards Manual* published by our division. Just three months ago, you founded the Document Design Department. Since then, the corporate response has been overwhelming for a set of corporate standards for the design of manuals.

Our enclosed report meets that demand. With sections on writing requirements—as well as content, revision, production, and graphic standards—the manual will increase Central Wyoming's ability to serve its growing number of clients.

Thank you for your support. I hope the document meets with your approval.

DOCUMENT 10: TITLE PAGE

Document Standards Manual
for
Central Wyoming Bank

December 21, 19XX

Prepared by
August Plata
Document Design Department

DOCUMENT 11: ABSTRACT

Central Wyoming Bank has expanded its services greatly over the past two years. To meet the growing demands for recording and analyzing data, the Document Design Department developed a number of new software programs.

Since these programs require user's manuals for their operation, it is appropriate that Central Wyoming Bank founded its first technical writing division, the Document Design Department. With a staff of four full-time technical writers, the Department will be able to produce the kind of quality user's manuals which will assure that our customers are served well and that our data maintain their integrity.

The following document delineates a set of company standards developed by the Document Design Department. Since the Department will coordinate the development of all user's manuals, it is important that individual software documentation developed by various divisions within the Central Wyoming Bank system be written according to uniform standards.

Four areas of document design are presented:

Writing Requirements: This section specifies techniques for creating a successful user's manual.

Content Standards: This section specifies the organizational plan of all Central Wyoming Bank user's manuals.

Revision Standards: This section specifies the procedure for creating and updating manuals.

Production Standards: This section specifies publication standards for creating user's manuals.

Graphic Standards: This section specifies the design standards for user's manuals.

With a goal of uniformity in the planning, production, and revision of user's manuals, the following standards will help Central Wyoming Bank employees perform their jobs with reliability and accuracy.

DOCUMENT 12: THE TABLE OF CONTENTS

57

Contents

Abstract ii
1.0   The Need for Document Standards A-1
1.1   Growth of Central Wyoming Bank...............A-3
1.2   Kinds of Software Development A-6
1.3   Kinds of User's Manuals A-8

2.0   Writing Requirements B-1
2.1   Audience Analysis Techniques B-4
2.1.1   Clerical B-7
2.1.2   Specialists.....................................B-10
2.1.3   Non-Specialists B-12
2.2   Drafting the User's Manual B-14
2.3   Composing the User's Manual..................B-15
2.3.1   Style B-17
2.3.2   Tone B-19
2.4   Field Testing the User's Manual B-20
2.4.1   Analysis of Results B-24
2.5   Revising the User's Manual B-26

3.0   Content Standards C-1
3.1   Title Page C-2
3.2   Table of Contents C-3
3.3   Abstract C-5
3.4   Introduction C-6
3.5   Systems Overview C-7
3.6   Operations C-9
3.7   Systems Codes C-11
3.8   Error Messages C-13
3.9   Index..C-15

4.0   Revision Standards D-1
4.1   Original Pages D-3
4.2   Updated Pages D-4
4.3   Inserted Pages D-5
4.4   Updated Sections D-6

5.0   Production Standards E-1
5.1   Selecting Binders E-3
5.2   Reprinted Tabs E-5
5.3   Reproduction Quality.........................E-7
5.4   Assembly E-9
5.5   Distribution E-10
5.5.1   Internal.......................................E-12
5.5.2   External E-13

6.0   Graphic Standards F-1
6.1   Pictures F-3
6.2   Illustrations F-5
6.3   Layout...F-8
6.4   Typography F-10

Technical Writing In The Corporate World

DOCUMENT 13: LIST OF FIGURES

EXERCISE: COLLECTING MODEL TECHNICAL DOCUMENTS

Research in technical writing reveals that individuals learn to write in organizational settings by identifying and analyzing documents written by others within that organization. Once sample documents are found, discussion may follow on which kinds are most effective. Similar approaches and organizational structures may then be used by individuals in their own writing.

In this exercise, follow the four steps below in order to collect model documents in your own organization.

STEP 1. *Identify key types of documents.* Begin by discovering the most common types of documents written in your division. As you gather different kinds of documents, develop a classification plan.

STEP 2. *Locate individual samples of each type of writing.* This part of the process may be begun by simply asking colleagues for documents that they feel have worked for them. As you look over a document, formulate questions about why certain parts of the document worked for the writer.

STEP 3. *Evaluate the samples with your colleagues.* In a group meeting, distribute copies of what you believe to be a model of each kind of document. With the group, try to identify the characteristics that make each sample effective.

STEP 4. *Disseminate the models.* Now that the best samples have been gathered and their characteristics defined, distribute these key documents to others in your group. The models will enable your colleagues to identify criteria for effectiveness and shape their writing so that it best serves their purposes.

SECTION 3

EDITING THE
TECHNICAL DOCUMENT

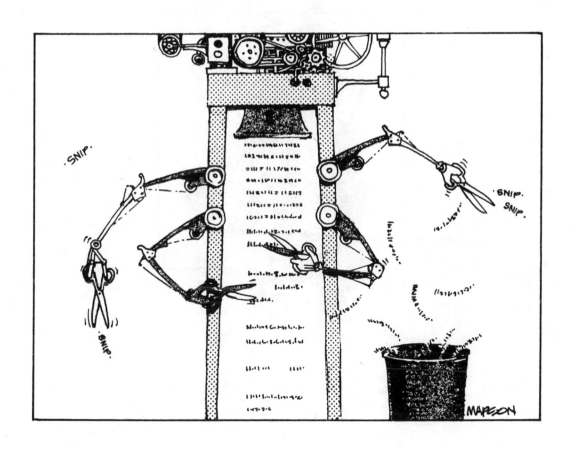

3.0 EDITING THE TECHNICAL DOCUMENT

In the first section of this book the focus was on defining technical writing. It helped you understand more clearly this unique kind of communication. In the second section the focus was on designing technical documents. It provided models of effective technical writing and posed questions about those models so that you might be more able to translate technical information. In this final section of this book let's turn to the editing of technical documents. It will enable you to evaluate your document and to revise those areas where lapses in organization, style, and correctness may have occurred.

3.1 ORGANIZATION

This book presents and analyzes a number of various forms of technical writing. Each kind of document has its own unique organizational pattern. It is, however, useful to generalize about the organizational characteristics of technical documents.

First, effective technical writing is highly *sectionalized*. While information in an academic essay or a scene in a novel may be presented over a number of pages, technical documents are divided into easily identifiable sections. Good technical writers ''chunk'' information so that readers can easily digest the information section by section. Hence, technical writers use headings and white spaces to that the complex technical information presented becomes easily accessible to busy readers.

Second, effective technical writing is highly *deductive*. Premises are stated clearly in technical documents, and conclusions are straightforwardly drawn. Ideas are not teased out over a number of pages but presented as quickly as possible. As a result of this deductive approach, readers are not lost, confused, or impatient with the material at hand.

Third, effective writing is *analytic*. Many forms of writing are descriptive or narrative. A poem, for example, may derive its force through its ability to convey a scene to a reader; or a historian may chronologically narrate a battle so that its outcome is clear. Technical writing, while it may use descriptive and narrative strategies, is first and foremost analytic. The overt purpose of a technical document is to analyze the situation at hand, to communicate technical information, and to create meaning for readers. Indeed, the deductive and sectionalized characteristics of technical writing are a direct result of the technical writer's goal to analyze complex information.

Therefore, as you put the finishing touches on a document, you might ask yourself the following questions about its organization:
1. Will my readers be able to scan the document and at once understand its overall structure?
2. Are the major points I need to make readily apparent to the reader?
3. Have I analyzed my subject so that my readers will be able to use the information?

3.2 STYLE

A recent bibliographic essay cites hundreds of articles dealing with style in technical communications. It might be imagined, then, that a definition of technical style might be given easily. No single definition, however, is satisfactory. Why?

This book began by defining technical writing as writing that explains technology to various technical, organizational, and societal audiences. Sometimes, these audiences must be addressed through different strategies, so it is impossible to talk about one kind of style in so complex a communications situation. Organization, length, sentence structure, word choice—all vary as communications situations shift.

Nevertheless, in any situation in which technical information must be conveyed, four broad characteristics of effective style may be identified:

1. *Reader awareness.* Technical writers realize that readers must absorb an enormous amount of detail in our information-based society. If there is any chance at all that complex information may be lost or misunderstood, the best technical writers take pains to convey that information to readers. As a result, effective technical writing is never obscure or confusing.

2. *Forcefulness.* The best technical writing avoids passive voice, weak word choice, or confused sentences. Instead, effective technical writing is marked by its forcefulness and its conviction. While technical writers rarely use the first person or needlessly insert their subjective views, they should have a sense of voice. Technical writers seek to control information, not to be controlled by it.

3. *Translatability.* Whether a technical specialist is writing to another specialist or to a non-specialist, every effort is made to analyze difficult information. An effective technical writer makes use of a number of translation strategies such as the use of diagrams and tables, frequent closure and explanation, and similes and analogies. Technical writing should clarify through analysis rather than obscure through complexity.

4. *Self-Sufficiency.* Ultimately, the most able technical writers create documents that stand independently. Instead of relying upon the transient knowledge of others in a group or upon filed documents, technical writers strive to present information that can be understood regardless of context. Technical writers realize that their audiences will shift radically with the passage of time. As personnel shift the backbone of an organization rests in its documents, and the information in these must be accessible regardless of time and circumstance.

As you edit your documents, you might ask yourself questions such as these regarding style:

1. If there is any chance that information in my document may be confusing, what precautions have I taken to assure that the information is lucidly presented?
2. Have I presented my information so straightforwardly that there is no doubt of my command of the subject?
3. If there are any especially difficult passages in my document, how have I handled these passages so that they may be understood by non-specialists?
4. If my document were to be read by someone not in my group, would the essence of the document be understood?

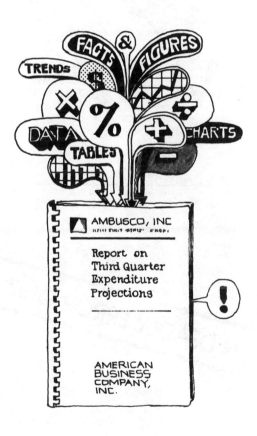

3.3 CORRECTNESS

So far, macro editing strategies have been discussed. As well, micro editing must be a part of finalizing the technical document. Concern over correctness usually centers on grammar and mechanics, therefore let's identify seven deadly errors of technical writing.

To assess your ability to recognize these errors, complete the brief exercise on the facing page; then check your answers against the key on page 68.

SEVEN DEADLY ERROR QUIZ

(Note: For book-length quides to strengthen your basic writing skills, see Susan L. Brock's *Better Business Writing* and Jack Swenson's *Writing Fitness*. Both may be ordered from the list in the back of this book.)

EXERCISE: IDENTIFYING THE SEVEN DEADLY ERRORS OF TECHNICAL WRITING

After reading each passage below, identify the error and correct it.

1. Each engineer must submit the designated log at the end of the day. They should also submit a copy of the test conductor worksheet.

Error: _____

Revision: _____

_____

2. The procedure on all IGRA graphic systems, each of which has multiple steps, have only one page of procedural documentation.

Error: _____

Revision: _____

_____

3. T47051 is at the warehouse but was not on your listing. This will be shipped to Atlanta with the other units currently at Edison.

Error: _____

Revision: _____

_____

4. Manning the tracking controls, passes over Area 21F will be tracked in real time.

Error: _____

Revision: _____

_____

5. A study was conducted concerning the effectiveness of our marketing approaches.

Error: _____

Revision: _____

_____

6. The DC21 converter which is powered by the system's on-board computer is integrated into Program 21C on the spacecraft.

Error: _____

Revision: _____

_____

7. There is one major concern for our division; to be sure that we upgrade the 21C Computer.

Error: _____

Revision: _____

_____

CORRECTNESS (Continued)

IDENTIFYING THE SEVEN DEADLY ERRORS OF TECHNICAL WRITING KEY

1. *Error:* Pronoun reference agreement problem
   Correction: Each engineer must submit the designated log at the end of the day. *He or she* should also submit a copy of the test conductor worksheet.
   Reference: 3.3.1

2. *Error:* Subject-verb agreement problem
   Correction: The procedure on all IGRA graphic systems, each of which has multiple steps, *has* only one page of procedural documentation.
   Reference: 3.3.2

3. *Error:* Vague pronoun reference
   Correction: T47051 is at the warehouse but was not on your listing. *This 450 pound piece of equipment* will be shipped to Atlanta with the other units currently at Edison.
   Reference: 3.3.3

4. *Error:* Dangling modifier
   Correction: Manning the tracking controls, *communications personnel* will track passes over Area 21F in real time.
   Reference: 3.3.4

5. *Error:* Overuse of passive voice
   Correction: *Research 500 conducted* a study concerning the effectiveness of our marketing approaches.
   Reference: 3.4.5

6. *Error:* Inappropriate comma use
   Correction: The DC21 converter, which is powered by the system's on-board computer, is integrated into Program 21C on the spacecraft.
   Reference: 3.3.6

7. *Error:* Inappropriate semicolon use
   Correction: There is one major concern for our division: to be sure that we upgrade the 21C Computer.
   Reference: 3.3.7

3.3.1 Pronoun Reference Agreement Problems

Pronouns must always agree with their antecedents. Pronouns such as *anyone, each, either, everyone, everybody, neither, nobody, none, no one, one,* and *somebody* are all singular. Therefore, by writing "each engineer" you limit yourself to referring to "he or she" later in your document. Since this kind of reference is the cause of many sexist constructions—engineers, for instance, always referred to as "he"—it is better simply to pluralize the noun in the first place. By this method, #1 in the above Exercise would be written as follows: "Engineers must submit the designated log at the end of the day. *They* should also submit a copy of the test conductor worksheet."

3.3.2 Subject-Verb Agreement Problems

Subjects and verbs must agree in number and person. However, intervening elements in a sentence often distract readers from identifying the subject (who or what the sentence is about) and its verb (the action of the subject). The writer of sentence #2 in the Exercise probably was confused by the plural noun "steps," and thus selected a plural verb.

In order to avoid this error, simply identify the subject, decide whether it is singular (*I, you, he, she* or *it*) or plural (*we, you,* or *they*), ignore any intervening nouns, and select the corresponding singular or plural verb.

3.3.3 Vague Pronoun Reference

Pronouns must clearly refer to their antecedents; remote or indefinite pronoun references break down coherence between sentences. The writer of sentence #3 would possibly mislead a reader into expecting a piece of paper—the listing—rather than a massive piece of equipment!

To avoid this sort of error, whenever you use the words *this, which,* or *it,* be sure you can identify a precise reference to a specific noun. If you cannot, supply an appropriate noun after the pronoun: "The civil engineering crew encountered a number of large boulders. This *situation* resulted in a delay in construction."

CORRECTNESS (Continued)

3.3.4 Dangling Modifiers

Verbal phrases often come at the beginning of sentences. When they do, they should refer clearly to the subject of the sentence.

Because writers so often use the passive voice in technical writing, subjects are often buried. As a result, verbal phrases dangle. The writer of sentence #4, for instance, does not specify who is manning the controls.

A simple way to correct this kind of error is to ask "who" or "what" is performing the action described in the phrase; if a noun is not present to answer the question, supply one: "After meeting the required deadline ("who met the deadline?"), *we* decided to continue immediately to the next phase of the project."

3.3.5 Overuse of Passive Voice

If the subject of a sentence performs the action of a sentence, then we say that sentence is written in active voice. If the subject is the receiver of the action of a sentence, then that sentence is written in passive voice. In the Exercise, sentence #5 is written in the passive voice. The revision in the Key is written in active voice.

Overuse of the passive voice tends to break down the readability of sentences and often leaves too many questions unanswered. Consider this sentence: "A significant report was written on December 17." Who wrote the report? Are our readers to spend time finding out? While it is sometimes necessary to use the passive voice—when, for instance, emphasis should be on an object or an idea—it is a mistake to use this type of construction remorselessly.

3.3.6 Inappropriate Comma Use

It is a mistake to use a comma simply because you think your reader will need a pause or you believe it sounds like a comma is needed. Instead, you should follow the four rules below for comma use within sentences. If you cannot think of one of these reasons, then do not use the comma:
1. To separate words or phrases in a series: "Terminals, printers, and screens, must all be redistributed."
2. To separate sentences joined by coordinate conjunctions (*and, but, or, nor, for, so,* and *yet*): "Some structures were carrying heavy and tall pressure vessels, *and* some were carrying vibrating machinery."
3. To set off introductory elements: (A) "*In fact,* the regression analysis proved quite useful." (B) *Although problems hampered the experiment,* I still consider it successful."
4. To set off nonrestrictive (additional) elements: The 3.5 inch 1.44Mb disk drive, *which was purchased last month,* appears to be convenient and reliable."

3.3.7 Inappropriate Semicolon Use

Usually, the semicolon (;) is used to give sentence variety. Used between two sentences, the semicolon can create a smooth transition for readers as they move from one clause to another.

To avoid the misuse of semicolons, simply make sure that a complete sentence exists on either side of the punctuation. In addition, be sure not to confuse semicolons with colons (:). Remember that a colon is used to call attention to a special item or to introduce a list: "The vendors include the following: Vitacom, Coastcom, and Megacorp." A semicolon is used to provide transition: "The company's business is the design and the construction of petrochemical processes; *therefore*, the primary activity of each engineering section must be focused accordingly." (For a list of adverbial conjunctions, see Section 1.2.)

3.4 A NOTE ON EDITING

Macro and micro editing are important parts of the technical writing process. Without proofreading, a document is likely to seem hastily prepared. If carefully proofread, a document will not have its information obscured or its readers distracted by errors.

Many writers often take this final part of the technical writing process to be the only part of the process and, as a result, become inhibited in their writing fluency and obsessed with matters of correctness. Although correctness is important, remember that there must be a well-organized document to edit in the first place. If you understand the demands of your situation and select the appropriate design strategy, then the editing process will allow you to refine your writing so that it will be free of distracting errors.

SECTION 4

CONCLUSION: THE IMPORTANCE OF TECHNICAL WRITING

4.0 CONCLUSION: THE IMPORTANCE OF TECHNICAL WRITING

Technical writing is more than a skill, more than an activity to be practiced in support of science or engineering. The ability to write about technical activities is the key to the success of the individual in the marketplace. In closing, we offer three reasons why you should invest the time to become an excellent technical writer.

First, the act of writing will allow you to clarify and refine your ideas. As you write, you begin to think more carefully and more precisely. Seen in this light, writing becomes a way of learning about your work. The more you write in formal and informal ways, the more fully you will understand the complexities of your profession.

Second, the ability to write well will allow you to be in control of your work environment. If you can write well about your projects, you will be able to create a frame of reference in which your efforts will be better understood. In essence, you will begin to play a part in shaping your organization through your use of language. Rather than being controlled by others, you will be in control.

Third, technical writing will allow you to inform your organization about your work. Many corporate and government ventures fail not because of technical problems but because of a failure to communicate those problems and thus find viable solutions. The modern organization depends on effective communications. Only by training yourself to be an excellent writer in your field will you be able to participate in molding the future of your organization and the larger society it serves.

APPENDICES

APPENDIX A: BUILDING A COMMUNITY OF TECHNICAL EDITORS

Throughout this book we have stressed the necessity of peer review. In order to produce effectively designed documents under tight time constraints, you must have others review your work before it is submitted.

To develop an environment in which members of your group may review each other's documents, begin by adopting the following principles:

1. *Throw away the school teacher's red pen.* As we have shown, the achievement of effective technical writing is a tough task. It is, therefore, useless to reduce effective technical writing to a matter of micro editing. Once the complexities and the difficulties involved in creating effective technical documents are acknowledged, there is a better chance that the subtleties of technical writing may be addressed as documents are read by your peers.

2. *Identify model documents.* Writing improves when sample documents are analyzed and criteria for effectiveness are established. As you begin to develop a community of peer reviewers, the first step is to find the best examples of documents written by your group and to discuss why these documents are effective.

3. *Develop precise questions for your readers.* When you give your document to someone for peer review, attach a list of five or six questions that you would like answered. If, for example, your reader can tell you that she was lost on page 2 or that another persuasive strategy might be more effective on page 6, then your document will be stronger than it would be if only a vague comment ("Seems good to me...") were offered.

4. *Make time for revision.* If a peer system is established, it will do your group little good if no time is allowed for revision. While this step means that documents may have to be planned ahead of deadline, carefully executed revision yields the strongest documents.

APPENDIX B: WORD PROCESSING FOR THE TECHNICAL WRITER

The development of word processing has increased the ease of creating effective documents. While word processing is not a magic aid to better writing, the techniques and advantages of word processing will allow you these benefits:

Greater document control. Writing with a word processor allows you control over your documents from the planning stage to the editing stage. Remember creating outlines on legal sheets, handwriting first drafts, typing the drafts, revising the typed copy, and re-typing the final copy? Now the planning, drafting, and revision stages can be completed on a word processor in a fraction of the time consumed by handwriting and typing.

Increased fluency. Once you master the best word processing program for your needs, your fluency will increase dramatically. Initial drafts will proceed more quickly, and final products will be submitted more promptly because of the confidence that comes from ease of revision.

Ease of revision. Revision is a time-consuming process, often involving re-typing a document. With word processing, however, revision can be accomplished in moments, and a fresh document incorporating your changes can be printed in seconds.

Enhanced collaborative writing. Once group-written documents had to be typed, reproduced, critiqued, and re-typed; now word-processed documents can be revised by a group gathered in front of a terminal. Even the longest documents can be drafted and edited by all members of a group in record time.

Enhanced professional appearance. Setting type is an expensive and time-consuming process; yet documents requiring a professional appearance can now be produced on desktop publishing equipment to rival even the most sophisticated printing process.

While it takes some time to become accustomed to computer-assisted writing, the time spent will be well worth your while.

APPENDIX C: TECHNICAL WRITING AND ENGLISH AS A SECOND LANGUAGE

More than 50% of all foreign college students declare majors in science and technology, and it is estimated that in the 1990s over half a million foreign students will be studying technologically related subjects. As these students graduate and take their places in American organizations, they will face unique communications situations. In addition, as the European common market opens and adds a greater sense of internationalism to organizations, non-native speakers and writers will be encountered with increasing regularity.

How can those who do not command English as their first language benefit by writing instruction? The following procedural guidelines will prove helpful:

Step 1. *Adopt an attitude of inquiry toward the learner.* The various language and cultural backgrounds of your colleagues will mean that their initial ability to write effective documents will differ. Try to discover the kinds of problems and successes that your ESL (English as a Second Language) colleagues encounter and discover ways to address their problems and acknowledge their successes.

Step 2. *Identify the levels of writing competency you wish attained.* All ESL employees should not be grouped together when you are judging their writing ability. Do you want someone to begin to learn the fundamentals of English syntax and vocabulary? Do you want someone to be able to write lab reports for technical audiences? To write reports for multiple audiences? It is important that you identify basic, intermediate, and advanced competency levels so that your ESL colleagues will know how they may attain mastery of these levels.

Step 3. *Develop an overall instructional plan.* While some corporations have an instructional curriculum for ESL employees, many lack a plan. Shortly after setting a level of mastery for your colleagues, discover ways to help them meet their goals. Apprenticeships to more advanced ESL employees and formal college courses are but two ways of establishing instructional plans. (For more information about ESL instruction, write Teachers of English to Speakers of Other Languages [TESOL], 1600 Cameron Street, Suite 300, Alexandria, Virginia, 22314.)

Step 4. *Provide frequent opportunities for writing.* Since we learn to write by writing, it is in the best interest of the ESL employee to write as much as possible and to have that writing assessed. With practice, ESL writers will gain confidence and increase their abilities to produce effective technical documents.

APPENDIX D: FOR FURTHER READING

As engineering began to flourish after World War II, technical writing became a profession in response to a need for those who could translate technical information for a variety of audiences. As corporations began to form departments of technical writing, the profession of technical writing grew.

Today, interest in technical writing is enormous. We offer the following selected list of sources for those wishing to know more about the field of technical writing.

Professional Societies:

American Business Communication Association, University of Illinois, English Building, 608 South Wright Street, Urbana, IL 61801.

Association of Teachers of Technical Writing, Department of Technical Communications, Clarkson College, Potsdam, NY 13676.

Society for Technical Communications, 815 15th Street, NNW, Washington, DC 20005.

Bibliographical Guides:

Moran, Michael G. and Deborah Journet, eds. *Research in Technical Communication: A Bibliographic Sourcebook.* Westbrook, CT: Greenwood Press, 1985.

Sides, Charles H. *Technical and Business Communication: Bibliographic Essays for Teachers and Corporate Trainers.* Urbana, IL: NCTE; Washington, DC: STC, 1989.

Readers:

Estrin, Herman A. *Technical and Professional Writing: A Practical Anthology.* New York: Preston Publishing Co., 1976.

Odell, Lee and Dixie Goswami, eds. *Writing in Nonacademic Settings.* New York: Guilford Press, 1985.

Handbook:

Brusaw, Charles T., Gerald J. Alred, and Walter E. Oliu. *Handbook of Technical Writing.* 3rd ed. New York: St. Martin's Press, 1987.

Word Processing:

Mitchell, Joan P. *Writing With a Computer*. Dallas: Houghton Mifflin Co., 1989.

ESL Instruction:

Hucken, Thomas N. and Leslie A. Olson. *English for Science and Technology: A Handbook for Nonnative Speakers*. New York: McGraw-Hill, 1983.

Technology Studies:

Marcus, Alan I. and Howard P. Segal. *Technology in America: A Brief History*. New York: Harcourt Brace Jovanovich, 1989.

Pacey, Arnold. *The Culture of Technology*. Cambridge, MA: MIT Press, 1983.

NOTES

Now Available From

Books•Videos•CD-ROMs•Computer-Based Training Products

If you enjoyed this book, we have great news for you. There are over 200 books available in the ***Crisp Fifty-Minute™ Series***.
For more information contact

Course Technology
25 Thomson Place
Boston, MA 02210
1-800-442-7477
www.courseilt.com

Subject Areas Include:

Management
Human Resources
Communication Skills
Personal Development
Marketing/Sales
Organizational Development
Customer Service/Quality
Computer Skills
Small Business and Entrepreneurship
Adult Literacy and Learning
Life Planning and Retirement